Numbers: Their Occult Power and Mystic Virtues

By

William Wynn Westcott

PREFACE TO THE FIRST EDITION, 1890.

SEVEN years have passed since this essay was written, and the MSS. pages have been lent to many friends and students of mystic lore and occult meanings. It is only at the earnest request of these kindly critics that I have consented to publish this volume. The contents are necessarily of a fragmentary character, and have been collected from an immense number of sources; the original matter has been intentionally reduced to the least possible quantity, so as to obtain space for the inclusion of the utmost amount of ancient, quaint and occult learning. It is impossible to give even an approximate list of works which have been consulted; direct quotations have been acknowledged in numerous instances, and (perhaps naturally) many a statement might have been equally well quoted from the book of a contemporary author, a mediæval monk, a Roman historian, a Greek poet, or a Hindoo Adept: to give the credit to the modern author would not be fair to the ancient sage, to refer the reader to a Sanskrit tome would be in most cases only loss of time and waste of paper. My great difficulty has been to supply information mystic enough to match the ideal of the work, and yet not so esoteric as to convey truths which Adepts have still concealed.

I must apologise for the barbarous appearance of foreign words, but it was not found practicable to supply Sanskrit, Coptic, Chaldee and Greek type, so the words have had to be transliterated. Hebrew and Chaldee should of course be read from right to left, and it was at first intended so to print them in their converted form, but the appearance of Hebrew in English letters reversed was too grotesque; ADNI is a representation of the Aleph, daleth, nun, yod, of "Adonai," but INDA would have been sheer barbarity: in the case of Hebrew words I have often added the pronunciation.

The "Secret Doctrine" of H. P. Blavatsky, a work of erudition containing a vast fund of archaic doctrine, has supplied me with valuable quotations. If any readers desire a deeper insight into the analogies between numbers and ideas, I refer them in addition to the works of Eliphaz Lévi, Athanasius Kircher, Godfrey Higgins, Michael Maier, and John Heydon; I have quoted from each of these authorities, and Thomas Taylor's "Theoretic Arithmetic" has supplied me with a great part of the purely arithmetical notions of the Pythagoreans, the elucidation of which was mainly due to him. In conclusion, I request my readers,—

Aut perlege et recte intellige,
Aut abstine a censura.

W. WYNN WESTCOTT.

PREFACE TO THE SECOND EDITION, 1902.

THE first edition of this little book has been long out of print, and for several years I have been asked to enlarge it, but until the present time sufficient leisure has not been found to collect the additional matter which seemed desirable.

This essay on Numbers now appears as Volume IX. of my Series entitled "Collectanea Hermetica," of which it seems to form a suitable part, and I am hopeful that it may be as well received by students of mystic philosophy as the previous volumes which treated of Alchemy, in the Hermetic Arcanum, Hermetic Art, Euphrates and Aesch Metzareph; the Dream of Scipio and the Golden verses of the Pythagoreans, the Pymander of Hermes and Egyptian Magic.

I have added in this edition many notes on the notions of the Rabbis of Israel, both from those who contributed to the Mishnah and Gemara of the Talmuds of Jerusalem and of Babylon, and from the Rabbis who made special study of the Kabalah. Only a few Talmudic treatises have as yet appeared in the English language, and hardly any Kabalistic tracts, except three from the Zohar or Book of Splendour, viz., the Siphra Dtzenioutha, the Idra Rabba and the Idra Suta. A few others are to be read in German and French translations. Many Talmudic and Kabalistic quotations may, however, be found in J. P. Stehelin's Rabbinical Literature of 1748; in John Allen's "Modern Judaism," 1816, and in works on the Kabalah by Adolph Franck and Christian Ginsburg, while Hershon has published Hebraic lore in his "Talmudic Miscellany," and "Genesis according to the Talmud."

The "Midrash ha Zohar" of D. H. Joel, Leipzig, 1849, narrates the relation between the Kabalah and Platonism, Neo-Platonism, Greek philosophy and the Zoroastrian doctrines of the Parsees.

Perhaps the oldest extant Kabalistic Book is the "Sepher Yetzirah," or "Book of Formation," an English translation of which has appeared in three editions from the Author's own pen. The fundamentals of the numerical Kabalistic ideas on creation are laid down in that treatise; it has also been printed both in French and German, and there is an American edition.

Upon the mathematical aspect of Numbers, readers may consult for further detail the works of Gauss, "Disquisitiones Arithmeticæ," 1801; Legendre, "Théorie des Nombres," 1830; W. G. O. Smith, "Reports on the Theory of Numbers," in the "Transactions of the British Association," 1859; James Ozanam, "Mathematical Recreations," 1710, translated by Hutton in 1814; Snart, "The Power of Numbers"; and Barlow's "Investigations of the Theory of Numbers."

For further information on Hindoo philosophy, see "The Theosophical Glossary" of H. P. Blavatsky, the works of Tukaram Tatya, and modern translations of the Vedas, Puranas and Upanishads, also Rama Prasad's "Nature's Finer Forces."

"Lamaism in Tibet," 1895, by Dr Laurence Austine Waddell, is a very learned work; it contains a vast store of information on the numerical occult lore of the Lamas and Buddhists.

Upon Egyptian Numbers consult the works of E. A. Wallis Budge; Flinders Petrie; Sir John Gardner Wilkinson; "Life in Ancient Egypt," by Adolf Erman; and "Egyptian Belief," by James Bonwick. Mystics will find much food for thought in the Yi-King, a very curious product of ancient Chinese lore. The Gnostic philosophy has a deep numerical basis, and the works of C. W. King and G. R. S. Mead may be suitably studied.

Many volumes of "Bijou Notes and Queries" have been published by S. C. Gould of Manchester, U.S.A., and these are full of numerical ideas.

I am prepared to find that critics will declare this volume to be an undigested collection of heterogeneous information, still I prefer to leave the data in their present form; for there is a scheme of instruction running through it, which will be recognised by students of certain schools, and others will be able to find a basis for a general knowledge of numbers viewed from the standpoint of occult science.

W. W. W.

PREFACE TO THE THIRD EDITION, 1911.

A FEW corrections have been made, and interesting notes have been added; many of these have been supplied by my pupils and fellow-students of the Rosicrucian Society.

W. W. W.

NUMBERS THEIR OCCULT POWER AND MYSTIC VIRTUES

PART I. PYTHAGORAS, HIS TENETS AND HIS FOLLOWERS

PYTHAGORAS, one of the greatest philosophers of ancient Europe, was the son of Mnesarchus, an engraver. He was born about the year 580 B.C., either at Samos, an island in the Ægean Sea, or, as some say, at Sidon in Phoenicia. Very little is known of his early life, beyond the fact that he won prizes for feats of agility at the Olympic Games. Having attained manhood and feeling dissatisfied with the amount of knowledge to be gained at home, he left his native land and spent many years in travel, visiting in turn most of the great centres of Learning. History narrates that his pilgrimage in search of wisdom extended to Egypt, Hindostan, Persia, Crete and Palestine, and that he gathered from each country fresh stores of information, and succeeded in becoming well acquainted with the Esoteric Wisdom as well as with the popular exoteric knowledge of each.

He returned with his mind well stored and his judgment matured, to his home, intending to open there a College of learning, but this he found to be impracticable owing to the opposition of its turbulent ruler Polycrates. Failing in this design, he migrated to Crotona, a noted city in Magna Græcia, which was a colony founded by Dorians on the South coast of Italy. It was here that this ever-famous Philosopher founded his College or Society of Students, which became known all over the civilized world as the central assembly of the learned of Europe; and here it was in secret conclave that Pythagoras taught that occult wisdom which he had gathered from the Gymnosophists and Brahmins of India, from the Hierophants of Egypt, the Oracle of Delphi, the Idæan cave, and from the Kabalah of the Hebrew Rabbis and Chaldean Magi. For nearly forty years he taught his pupils, and exhibited his wonderful powers; but an end was put to his institution, and he himself was forced to flee from the city, owing to a conspiracy and rebellion which arose on account of a quarrel between the people of Crotona and the inhabitants of Sybaris: he succeeded in reaching Metapontum, where he is said to have died about the year 500 B.C.

Among the ancient authors from whom we derive our knowledge of the life and doctrines of Pythagoras and his successors, the following are notable:—

B.C. 450.—Herodotus, who speaks of the mysteries of the Pythagoreans as similar to those of Orpheus.

B.C. 394.—Archytas of Tarentum, who left a fragment upon Pythagorean Arithmetic.

B.C. 380.—Theon of Smyrna.

B.C. 370.—Philolaus. From three books of this author it is believed that Plato compiled his book Timæus; he was probably the first who committed to writing the doctrines of Pythagoras.

B.C. 322.—Aristotle. Refer to his "Metaphysica," "Moralia Magna," and "Nicomachean Ethics." Nicomachus of Stagyra was his father.

B.C. 276.—Eratosthenes, author of a work entitled "Kokkinon" or "Cribrum," a "Sieve to separate Prime from Composite Numbers."

B.C. 40.—Cicero. Refer to his works "De Finibus" and "De natura Deorum."

50 A.D.—Nicomachus of Gerasa; Treatises on Arithmetic and Harmony.

300 A.D.—Porphyry of Tyre, a great philosopher, sometimes named in Syriac, Melekh or King, was the pupil of Longinus and Plotinus.

340 A.D.—Jamblicus wrote "De mysteriis," "De vita Pythagorica," "The Arithmetic of Nicomachus of Gerasa," and "The Theological Properties of Numbers."

450 A.D.—Proclus, in his commentary on the "Works and Days" of Hesiod, gives information concerning the Pythagorean views of numbers.

560 A.D.—Simplicius of Cilicia, a contemporary of Justinian.

850 A.D.—Photius of Constantinople has left a Bibliotheca of the ideas of the older philosophers.

Coming down to more recent times, the following authors should be consulted:—Meursius, Johannes, 1620; Meibomius, Marcus, 1650; and Kircher, Athanasius, 1660. They collected and epitomized all that was extant of previous authors concerning the doctrines of the Pythagoreans. The first eminent follower of Pythagoras was Aristæus, who married Theano, the widow of his master: next followed Mnesarchus, the son of Pythagoras; and later Bulagoras, Tidas, and Diodorus the Aspendian. After the original school was dispersed, the chief instructors became Clinias and Philolaus at Heraclea; Theorides and Eurytus at Metapontum; and Archytas, the sage of Tarentum.

The school of Pythagoras had several peculiar characteristics. Every new member was obliged to pass a period of five years of contemplation in perfect silence; the members held everything in common, and rejected animal food; they were believers in the doctrine of metempsychosis, and were inspired with an ardent and implicit faith in their founder and teacher. So much did the element of faith enter into their training, that "*autos epha*"—"He said it"—was to them complete proof. Intense fraternal affection between the pupils was also a marked feature of the school; hence their saying, "my friend is my other self," has become a by-word to this day. The teaching was in a great measure secret, and certain studies and knowledge were allotted to each class and grade of instruction: merit and ability alone sufficed to enable anyone to pass to the higher classes and to a knowledge of the more recondite mysteries. No person was permitted to commit to writing any tenet, or secret doctrine, and, so far as is known, no pupil ever broke the rule until after his death and the dispersion of the school.

We are thus entirely dependent on the scraps of information which have been handed down to us from his successors, and from his and their critics. A considerable amount of uncertainty, therefore, is inseparable from any consideration of the real doctrines of Pythagoras himself, but we are on surer ground when we investigate the opinions of his followers.

It is recorded that his instruction to his followers was formulated into two great divisions—the science of numbers and the theory of magnitude. The former division included two branches, arithmetic and musical harmony; the latter was further subdivided into the consideration of magnitude at rest—geometry, and magnitude in motion—astronomy.

The most striking peculiarities of his doctrines are dependent on the mathematical conceptions, numerical ideas, and impersonations upon which his philosophy was founded.

The principles governing Numbers were supposed to be the principles of all Real Existences; and as Numbers are the primary constituents of Mathematical Quantities, and at the same time present many analogies to various realities, it was further inferred that the elements of Numbers were the elements of Realities. To Pythagoras himself it is believed that the natives of Europe owe the first teaching of the properties of Numbers, of the principles of music, and of physics; but there is evidence that he had visited Central Asia, and there had acquired the mathematical ideas which form the basis of his doctrine. The modes of thought introduced by Pythagoras, and followed by his successor Jamblicus and others, became known later on by the titles of the "Italian school," or the "Doric school."

The followers of Pythagoras delivered their knowledge to pupils, fitted by selection and by training to receive it, in secret; but to others by numerical and mathematical names and notions. Hence they called forms, numbers; a point, the monad; a line, the dyad; a superficies, the triad; and a solid, the tetrad.

Intuitive knowledge was referred to the Monad type.

Reason and causation ,, ,, Dyad type.

Imagination (form or rupa) ,, ,, Triad type.

Sensation of material objects ,, ,, Tetrad type.

Indeed, they referred every object, planet, man, idea and essence to some number or other, in a way which to most moderns must seem curious and mystical in the highest degree.

"The numerals of Pythagoras," says Porphyry, who lived about 300 A. D., "were hieroglyphic symbols, by means whereof he explained all ideas concerning the nature of things," and the same method of explaining the secrets of nature is once again being insisted upon in the new revelation of the "Secret Doctrine," by H. P. Blavatsky.

"Numbers are a key to the ancient views of cosmogony—in its broad sense, spiritually as well as physically considered, and to the evolution of the present human race; all systems of religious mysticism are based upon numerals. The sacredness of numbers begins with the Great First Cause, the One, and ends only with the nought or zero—symbol of the infinite and boundless universe." "Isis Unveiled," vol. ii. 407.

Tradition narrates that the students of the Pythagorean school, at first classed as Exoterici or Auscultantes, listeners, were privileged to rise by merit and ability to the higher grades of Genuini, Perfecti, Mathematici or the most coveted title of Esoterici.

HP Blavatsky

PART II. PYTHAGOREAN VIEWS ON NUMBERS

THE foundation of Pythagorean Mathematics was as follows:

The first natural division of Numbers is into EVEN and ODD, an EVEN number being one which is divisible into two equal parts, without leaving a monad between them. The ODD number, when divided into two equal parts, leaves the monad in the middle between the parts.

All even numbers also (except the dyad—two—which is simply two unities) may be divided into two equal parts, and also into two unequal parts, yet so that in neither division will either parity be mingled with imparity, nor imparity with parity. The binary number two cannot be divided into two unequal parts.

Thus io divides into 5 and 5, equal parts, also into 3 and 7, both imparities, and into 6 and 4, both parities; and 8 divides into 4 and 4, equals and parities, and into 5 and 3, both imparities.

But the ODD number is only divisible into uneven parts, and one part is also a parity and the other part an imparity; thus 7 into 4 and 3, or 5 and 2, in both cases unequal, and odd and even.

The ancients also remarked the monad to be "odd," and to be the first "odd number," because it cannot be divided into two equal numbers. Another reason they saw was that the monad, added to an even number, became an odd number, but if evens are added to evens the result is an even number.

Aristotle, in his Pythagoric treatise, remarks that the monad partakes also of the nature of the even number, because when added to the odd it makes the even, and added to the even the odd is formed.

Hence it is called "evenly odd." Archytas of Tarentum was of the same opinion.

The Monad, then, is the first idea of the odd number; and so the Pythagoreans speak of the "two" as the "first idea of the indefinite dyad," and attribute the number 2 to that which is indefinite, unknown, and inordinate in the world; just as they adapt the monad to all that is definite and orderly. They noted also that in the series of numbers from unity, the terms are increased each by the monad once added, and so their ratios to each other are lessened; thus 2 is 1 + 1, or double its predecessor; 3 is not double 2, but 2 and the monad, sesquialter; 4 to 3 is 3 and the monad, and the ratio is sesquitertian; the sesquiquintan 6 to 5 is less also than its forerunner, the sesquiquartan 5 and 4, and so on through the series.

They also noted that every number is one half of the total of the numbers about it, in the natural series; thus 5 is half of 6 and 4. And also of the sum of the numbers again above and below this pair; thus 5 is also half of 7 and 3, and so on till unity is reached; for the monad alone has not two terms, one below and one above; it has one above it only, and hence it is said to be the "source of all multitude."

"Evenly even" is another term applied anciently to one sort of even numbers. Such are those which divide into two equal parts, and each part divides evenly, and the even division is continued until unity is reached; such a number is 64. These numbers form a series, in a duple ratio from unity; thus 1, 2, 4, 8, 16, 32. "Evenly odd," applied to an even number, points out that like 6, so, 14, and 28, when divided into two equal parts, these are found to be indivisible into equal parts. A series of these numbers is formed by doubling the items of a series of odd numbers, thus:

1, 3, 5, 7, 9 produce 2, 6, 10, 14, 18.

Unevenly even numbers may be parted into two equal divisions, and these parts again equally divided, but the process does not proceed until unity is reached; such numbers are 24 and 28.

Odd numbers also are susceptible of being looked upon from three points of view, thus:

"First and incomposite"; such are 3, 5, 7, 11, 13, 19, 23, 29, 31; no other number measures them but unity; they are not composed of other numbers, but are generated from unity alone.

"Second and composite" are indeed "odd," but contain and are composed from other numbers; such are 9, 15, 21, 25, 27, 33, and 39. These have parts which are denominated from a foreign number, or word, as well as proper unity, thus 9 has a third part which is 3; 15 has a third part which is 5; and a fifth part 3; hence as containing a foreign part, it is called second, and as containing a divisibility, it is composite.

The Third Variety of odd numbers is more complex, and is of itself second and composite, but with reference to another is first and incomposite; such are 9 and 25. These are divisible, each of them that is second and composite, yet have no common measure; thus 3 which divides the 9 does not divide the 25.

Odd numbers are sorted out into these three classes by a device, called the "Sieve of Eratosthenes," which is of too complex a nature to form part of a monograph so discursive as this must be.

Even numbers have also been divided by the ancient sages into Perfect, Deficient and Superabundant.

Superperfect or Superabundant are such as 12 and 24.

Deficient are such as 8 and 14.

Perfect are such as 6 and 28; equal to the number of their parts; as 28—half is 14, a fourth is 7, a seventh is 4, a fourteenth part is 2, and the twenty-eighth is 1, which quotients added together are 28.

In Deficient numbers, such as 14, the parts are surpassed by the whole: one seventh is 2, a half is 7, a fourteenth is 1; the aggregate is 10, or less than 14.

In Superabundant, as 12, the whole surpasses the aggregate of its parts; thus the sixth is 2, a fourth is 3, a third is 4, a half is 6, and a twelfth is 1; and the aggregate is 16, or more than 12.

Superperfect numbers they looked on as similar to Briareus, the hundred-handed giant: his parts were too numerous; the deficient numbers resembled Cyclops, who had but one eye; whilst the perfect numbers have the temperament of a middle limit, and are the emulators of Virtue, a medium between excess and defect, not the summit, as some ancients falsely thought.

Evil is indeed opposed to evil, but both to one good. Good, however, is never opposed to good, but to two evils.

The Perfect numbers are also like the virtues, few in number; whilst the other two classes are like the vices—numerous, inordinate, and indefinite.

There is but one perfect number between 1 and 10, that is 6; only one between 10 and 100, that is 28; only one between 100 and 1000, that is 496; and between 1000 and 10,000 only one, that is 8128.

Odd numbers they called Gnomons, because, being added to squares, they keep the same figures as in Geometry: see Simplicius, liber 3.

A number which is formed by the multiplication of an odd and an even number together they called Hermaphrodite, or "arrenothelus."

In connection with these notes on parity and imparity, definite and indefinite numbers, it is to be noted that the old philosophers were deeply imbued with the union of numerical ideas with Nature—in its common acceptation, and also to the natures, essences or substrata of things.

The nature of good to them was definite, that of evil indefinite; and the more indefinite the nature of the evil, the worse it was. Goodness alone can define or bound the indefinite. In the human soul exists a certain vestige of divine goodness (Buddhi); this bounds and moderates the indefiniteness and inequality of its desires.

It may be demonstrated that all inequality arises from equality, so that obtaining, as it were, the power of a mother and a root, she pours forth with exuberant fertility all sorts of inequality; and did space and time allow, it could be also shown that all inequality may be reduced to equality.

Iamblichus, in his treatise on the Arithmetic of Nicomachus, throws another light on numbers; he says some are like friends, they are Amicable numbers, as 284 and 220.

Pythagoras, being asked what a friend was, said ἕτερος εγω = "another I." Now this is demonstrated to be the case in these numbers; the parts of each are generative of each other, according to the nature of friendship.

Ozanam, a French mathematician, A.D. 1710, gives examples in his "Mathematical Recreations" of such Amicable Numbers. He remarks that 220 is equal to the sum of the aliquot parts of 284; thus $1 + 2 + 4 + 71 + 142 = 220$: and 284 is equal to the sum of the aliquot parts of 220; thus $1 + 2 + 4 + 5 + 10 + 11 + 20 + 22 + 44 + 55 + 110 = 284$.

Another such pair of numbers are 17,296 and 18,416.

Ozanam

Very curious speculations as to the relation between Numbers and marriage, and the character of offspring from it, are to be found scattered through the writings of the Philosophers. Plato, in his "Republic," has a passage concerning a geometric number, which, divinely generated, will be fortunate or unfortunate. Nicomachus also speaks of this same number, and he calls it the Nuptial Number; and he passes from it to state that from two good parents only good offspring can come; from two bad parents only bad; and from a good and a bad parent only bad; whence he warns the Republic against wedlock in a confused or disorderly manner, from which, the progeny being depraved, discord will result. Simplicius, in his commentary on the 2nd Book of Aristotle, "On the Heavens," remarks that Pythagoras and his followers claimed to have heard the Music of the Spheres, to have heard an harmonic sound produced by the motion of the planets, and from the sound

to have calculated by numbers the ratio of distance and size of the Sun, Moon, Venus and Mercury. To this Aristotle objected, but perhaps the difficulty might be solved: in this sublunary sphere all things are not commensurate, nor is everything sensible to every body alike. Animals can be scented, and their presence definitely known, by dogs when at great distances from them, and when man is in complete ignorance of their existence. Some of the ancients thought the soul had three vehicles—the terrestrial body, an aerial one in which it is punished, and an ethereal one, luminous and celestial, in which the soul abides when in a state of bliss. It may be that some one, by purification of the senses, by hereditary magical power, or by probity, or by the sacred operations of his religion, may perceive, with a terrestrial body laid aside, things imperceptible to us, and hear sounds inaudible to us still in bondage; or with mantle partly unfolded, some adept or truth-seeker may perceive, with eyes upraised, sights invisible to mortals, whilst yet his ears are deaf to the sounds beyond us both. For why do we see the stars, while yet we hear not their motion:

Why come not angels from the realms of glory
To visit earth, as in the days of old?
Is heaven more distant
Or has earth grown cold?

PART III. THE KABALAH ON NUMBERS

MANY nations of antiquity made use of the letters of their alphabets as substitutes for any independent signs to typify numerical conceptions. It is with the Hebrew letters as numerals that we are chiefly concerned, and to a smaller extent with the Greek. Ancient records show that the Greeks used their numbers almost exclusively for everyday purposes; while the Jewish Rabbis added to their practical value special peculiar purposes, and looked to them to furnish deeper views of nature, existence and doctrine. No doubt can exist that the ancient Egyptians were fully aware of the wondrous mysteries which numbers are able to disclose, so, considering that Greece, and neither Judea nor Babylon, succeeded to the empires of ancient Egypt, it is a curious fact how little knowledge of the dogmas of the Hierophants of Sais, Memphis and Thebes Greek literature has transmitted to us.

The Jewish Rabbis discovered so much of interest and importance behind the merely superficial value of numbers, and of words as their representatives, that they gradually developed a complete science of numerical conceptions apart from mathematics; this took the name of Kabalah or Qabalah, Cabbala, or even Cabala, words variously misspelt from QBLH— the Received doctrine, from the root QBL, meaning to Receive.

The Greeks as aforesaid did not develop nor use their letters as numbers for mental conceptions, yet in the Middle Ages we often find Greek letters used to transliterate Hebrew similars, and so there was formed a bastard Greek Kabalah on the Hebrew type.

It must be constantly borne in mind that all Hebrew words or numbers are read from right to left, or the reverse of English words; but in their English transliteration they are here in English order.

The corresponding numerals, Greek and Hebrew letters, are here given with their English names, and the English synonymous letters are also added.

A	B	G	D	H	U or V	Z
Aleph	Beth	Gimel	Daleth	Heh	Vau	Zain
y	ב	ג	ד	ה	ו	ז
1	2	3	4	5	6	7
Alpha	Beta	Gamma	Delta	Epsilon	*Episemon*	Zeta
α	β	γ	δ	ε	ς	ζ

Ch	Th	Y or I or J	K	L	M	N
Heth	Teth	Yod	Kaph	Lamed	Mem	Nun
ח	ט	׳	כ	ל	מ	נ
8	9	10	20	30	40	50
Eta	Theta	Iota	Kappa	Lambda	Mu	Nu
ε	θ	ι	κ	λ	μ	ν

S	O	P	Tz	Q	R
Samekh	Ayin	Peh	Tzaddi	Qoph	Resh
ס	y	פ	צ	ק	ר
60	70	80	90	100	200

Xi	Omicron	Pi	*Koppa*	Rho	Sigma
ξ	ο	π	ϙ	σ or ς	

Sh	T	K	M	N	
Shin	Tau	Final	Kaph	Final Mem	Final Nun
שׁ	ת	ך	ם	ן	
300	400	500	600	700	
Tau	Upsilon	Phi	Chi	Psi	
τ	υ	φ	χ	ψ	

P	Tz	
Final Peh	Final Tzaddi	Dotted Aleph
800	900	1000
Omega	Sanpi	Alpha dashed
ω	ͳ	ἀ

Note that there were no proper Greek Letters for 6, 90, and 900, so they used special symbols—*episemon* (vau, or bau, digamma) for 6; *koppa* for 90; and *sanpi* for 900—ς ϙ ͳ).

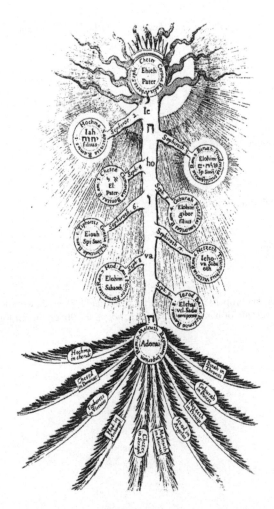

The Tree of Life

At some periods the five finals were not used for the hundreds, but instead Tau was written for 400 and other hundreds added; thus 500 was TQ. Another point of importance is that the Jews never write JH Jah for 15, because it is a Deity title, they use instead 9, 6 thus TV, teth vau. The Kabalists used JH only when they desired to call attention to the Holy Name in the number.

In certain Kabalistic numerical computations many Rabbis deemed it permissible to add an Aleph, one, and this they called the Colel.

In some cases we find the Greeks to have used their letters in direct order for purposes of numeration, as may be seen in some copies of very old poems (the 24 books of Homer's Iliad and Odyssey, for example), in which the stanzas bear the letters consecutively, in a similar manner to the Hebrew letters heading the portions of the 119th Psalm in our Bibles.

The word Kabalah includes the Hebrew Doctrines of Cosmogony and Theology as well as the Science of Numbers. The former is specified as the Dogmatic Kabalah, the latter as the Literal Kabalah.

By means of associating the ancient doctrines of Numbers with the letters of the alphabet, the Planets, Stars, Zodiacal signs and other astronomical terms, a form of divination became practised, by which the professors attempted to foretell the future, life and death, good and evil Fortune, detection of theft, etc., an ample explanation of which may be studied by the curious in the "Holy Guide" of John Heydon.

With this system is associated the practice of pure Astrology, the divination of Fate by means of the Heavenly bodies, especially the formation of the so-called Horoscopes—schemes of the arrangement of the Planets at the moment of Birth, from which all the important phases of the life can be inferred—by some few persons. The Kabalah became a means of handing down from one generation to another hidden truths, religious notions, secrets of nature, ideas of Cosmogony, and facts of history, in a form which was unintelligible to the uninitiated; and the revealing of the secrets, and the methods of interpretation were veiled in mystery, and only to be approached through Religion.

The more practical part of the system was involved in the three processes of:—

GEMATRIA, NOTARICON, and TEMURA.

Gematria, a method depending on the fact that each Hebrew letter had a numerical value. When the sum of the numbers of the letters composing a word was the same as the sum of the letters of another word, however different, they perceived an analogy between them, and considered them to have a necessary connection. Thus certain numbers got to be well known as meaning certain things; and not words only, but sentences were treated in this manner; thus, as an example referring to Genesis xviii. v. 2, we find the words, "and lo, three men," Vehennah, shalisha, VHNH SHLSHH; this set down in numbers becomes 6, 5, 50, 5, 300, 30, 300, 5, which amount to 701: now the words, "these are Michael, Gabriel, and Raphael," "Alu Mikhael Gabriel ve Raphael," ALU MIKAL GBRIAL V RPAL converted are, 1, 30, 6, 40, 10, 20, 1, 30, 3, 2, 200, 10, 1, 30, 6, 200, 80, 1, 30, also amounting to 701, and the Rabbis argued that these two sets of three beings were identical. Some Christian Kabalists point out that in Genesis xlix. v. 10 we find "Yebah Shiloh," YBA SHILH, "Shiloh shall come," which amount to 358; and that the word "Messiah," MShVCh is 40, 300, to, 8, or 358; but so is also Nachash, the Serpent of Moses, NChSh, 50, 8, 300; and I must remark that the claim to translate ShILh, or, as some ancient Hebrew MSS. write it, ShLh, by "Shiloh," in the sense of Jesus Christ, is far-fetched. The word is simply "rest," or "peace," in its simplest meaning, but also is the Scorpio of the Chaldean zodiac (related to Nachash, serpent); and "Judah," of whom Jacob is talking in the prophecy, is the sign of the zodiac; Leo for "Judah is a lion's whelp" (the Chaldean zodiac has a lion couchant), "he crouches as a lion." In this sense, then, "the sceptre shall not depart from Judah," *i.e.*, power shall not leave Leo, until Shelah, Shiloh or Scorpio shall come up or rise. Astronomy teaches that as Leo passes away from the meridian, Scorpio rises. The title "Comforter," "Menachem," MNChM, 40, 50, 8, 40, amounting to 138, and the title "The Branch," applied to the Messiah in Zechariah iii. v. 8, namely, TzMCh, 90, 40, 8, also 138, are of the same number. Metatron, the great angel MThRThN, and ShADDAI ShDI, translated "Almighty," are both 314. The letter Shin, Sh, = 300, is used as a glyph of "the spirit of the living gods," Ruach Elohim RUCh ALhIM, which transmutes into 200, 6, 8, 1, 30, 5, 10, 40, or 300.

The Kabalists sometimes considered the units to refer to Divine Beings, the tens to celestial bodies, hundreds to things of earth, and thousands to future events.

Notaricon, a word derived from the Latin *notarius*, a shorthand writer, means the construction of a word from the initial or final letters of the several words of a sentence; or vice versa the construction of a sentence of which each word in order begins with the several letters composing a given word: processes of contraction and expansion, therefore.

Refer to Deuteronomy xxx. V. 12, and find that Moses asks, "Who shall go up for us to heaven?" the initials of the words of the sentence, MY YOLh LNU HShMYMH, read "My yeolah lenu hashemimha," form the word MYLH or "Mylah," which means "Circumcision," and the final letters form the word Jehovah, YHUH or IHVH, suggesting that Jehovah pointed out the way, by circumcision, to heaven. Again the first six letters of the book of Genesis, BRAShIT, Berasit, translated "In the beginning," but more properly "In wisdom," are the initials of the words BRAShIT RAH ALHIM ShYQBLU IShRAL TURH, read "Berasit rauah Elohim shyequebelu Israel torah," which mean "In the beginning, God saw that Israel would accept the Law."

The famous Rabbinic name of power, "AGLA," is formed of the initials of the sentence, "Tu potens in sæculum Domine," ATH GBUR LOULM ADNI, Ateh gibur loulam Adonai. The word "Amen" is from AMN, the initials of "Adonai melekh namen," ADNI MLK NAMN, meaning "The Lord and Faithful King."

Temura means Permutation; sometimes the letters of a word are transposed according to certain rules, and with certain limitations; at others each letter of a word is replaced by another according to a definite scheme, forming a new word, of which permutation there are many recognised forms. For example, the alphabet of 22 letters is halved and the two sets placed one over the other in reverse order, thus:—

A	B	G	D	H	V	Z	Ch	Th	Y	K
T	Sh	R	Q	Tz	P	O	S	N	M	L

then A is changed to T, and V to P, and so on; so Babel = BBL becomes Sheshak, *i.e.*, ShShx used by Jeremiah xxv. v. 26. This form is called Atbash or AT-BSh; it will be seen that there must be 21 other possible forms, and these were named in order, thus, Albat, Agdat, etc.; the complete set was called "the combinations of Tziruph." Other Permutations were named Rational, Right, Averse and Irregular; these are produced by forming a square and subdividing it by 21 lines in each direction into 484 smaller squares, and then writing in each square a letter in order successively from right to left, or from above down, or the reverse. The most popular mode of permutation has however been the form called "Kabalah of the Nine Chambers," produced by the intersection of two horizontal and two vertical lines, forming nine spaces, a central square, and 4 three-sided figures, and 4 two-sided figures, to each of which are allotted certain letters; there are several modes even of this arrangement, and there is a mystical mode of allotting the Sephiroth to this figure, but this is a Rosicrucian secret.

This method is used in a superficial manner in Mark Master Masonry.

A further development of the Numerical Kabalah consists of arithmetical processes of Extension and Contraction; thus Tetragrammaton is considered as Y 10, H 5, V 6, H 5, or 26, but also may be spelled in full YVD 20, HA 6, VV 12, HA 6, or 44.

Again, the Kabalists extended a number by series. Zain Z or 7 becomes 1 and 2 and 3 and 4 and 5 and 6 and 7, or 28. After another manner they contracted, as 28 was equal to 2 and 8, or ro. Again, Tetragrammaton 26 became 2 and 6, or 8, so every number was reducible to a primary numeral. In this manner, within certain restrictive laws, every word had analogies with certain others; thus AB father 1 and 2 are 3, IHV Jehu 10 and 5 and 6 are 21, 2 and 1 are 3. AL ShDI, Al Shaddai, God Almighty, 1, 30, 300, 4, 10, or 345, becomes 12, and then 2 and 1 are 3; HVA or HOA 5, 6, 1, are 12, and then 3; and GDVLH Gedulah 3, 4, 6, 30, 5 are 48, and are 12 and 3.

Another method of substitution leading to results of an opposite character is the substitution in any word of similar letters of another group, hard for soft, or sibilant for dental; thus in TM = perfect, exchange Th for T, and obtain ThM, meaning defiled: ShAN, secure, tranquil, becomes SAN, battle; ShKL, wisdom, becomes SKL, foolish. In the word Shaddai, Sher, Almighty, with soft sibilant and soft dental is Shiddah, a wife; if we replace with a hard dental, a partial change of meaning is effected, ShThH, Sittah, an adulterous wife; both letters hardened completely change the sense, STh, Seth, a fallen man, a backslider; SThN, Satan, adversary.

I cannot, without Hebrew letters, explain well the change of sound in the Shin SH, from SH to S, but it is marked by a dot over the right or left tooth of the three teeth of the letter.

A deep mystery is concealed in the Genetic account of the conversion of the names of Abram, ABRM, into Abraham, ABRHM, and that of his wife Sarai, ShRI, into Sarah, SHRH, see Genesis xvii. v. 5–15, on the occasion of the conception of Isaac, YTZChQ or YShChQ, from the root ShChQ or TzChQ, "laugh," when Sarah was 90 and Abraham 100 years old. This was on the occasion of the covenant made by Jehovah with Abram, and the institution of circumcision of males in token thereof. Now here we have the addition of an H or 5, the essentially Female Letter, to the name of Abraham, and a conversion of a Yod into He, Y into H, in the case of Sarah; and then their sterility is destroyed.

Some learned men consider Abraham to be a conversion of Brahma, the Hindoo Deity. The name splits up curiously. AB is father, BR is son, AM is like OM or AUM, a deific name of Power; RM meant "he is lifted up." Blavatsky remarks that Abraham and Saturn were identical in Astro-symbology; the Father of the Pharisees was Jehovah, and they were of the seed of Abraham.

The number of ABRM is 1, 2, 200, 40 or 243, the number of the man figure, Seir Anpin, representing Microprosopus.

Read Pistorius, "Ars Cabalistica," for the effect of adding H 5 to men's names, see page 969; also Inman, "Ancient Faiths," article Abraham; "Secret Doctrine," i. 578, ii. 77; also C. W. King, "The Gnostics."

The name Sarah also has a curious set of similars in Hebrew—SRH, princess; SAR, flesh; SOR, gate; SChR, black; SUR, hairy seir; SRT, incision; SR and SRR, navel; and note the Sacti of Brahma is Sara-swati, watery; Sara refers to SRI, Lakhsmi, Aphrodite, and all are related to Water and Luna, Vach, Sophia of the Gnostics, and the ideal Holy Ghost, all feminine.

The 243 of Abram becomes 248 by adding H, and Sarai 510 becomes 505 by taking 5 off, putting H for Y, and the total of the two names is unaltered, being 753; 248 is the number of the members of Microprosopus and of RChM, rechem or Mercy.

Before leaving this subject, a reference must be made to the Magic Squares, of the Planets, etc.; to each planet belongs a special unit, and secondarily other numbers.

Thus the Square of Saturn has three compartments each way, and in each subdivision is a unit, 1 to 9, so arranged that the columns add up to 15 every way, the total being 45. The Square of Jupiter has a side of four divisions, total 16; each line adds up to 34, and the total is 136.

The Square of Mars is given here as an example, each side 5, total squares 25, each side counting 65, and total 325.

11	24	7	20	3
4	12	25	8	16
17	5	13	21	9
10	18	1	14	22
23	6	19	2	15

Similarly the four several numbers of Sol are 6, 36, 111, 666. Of Venus, 7, 49, 175, 1225. Of Mercury, 8, 64, 260, 2080.

Of Luna, 9, 81, 369, 3321. Each number then becomes a name. Take the case of Mercury; 64 is alike DIN and DNI, Din and Doni; 260 is Tiriel, TIRIAL; and 2080 is Taphthartharath, TPTRTRT.

Rawlinson, in his volumes on the Ancient Monarchies, states that the Chaldeans associated mystic numbers with their Deities; thus to Anu, Pluto, 60; Bel, Jupiter, 50; Hoa, Neptune, 40; Sin, the Moon, 30; Shamash, the Sun, 20; Nergal (Mars), 12; and Beltis or Mylitta, 15; and Nin is Saturn, 10.

It will be noticed that the great number of Sol is 666, called Sorath, SURT, the number of the Beast, about which so much folly has been written. One famous square of five times five divisions, amounting in most directions to 666, is formed of the mystic words *sator, arepo, tenet, opera, rotas*. Of these the first, third, and last number 666, but *opera* and its reverse number only 356. The number 608 is notable, being in Coptic, PhRE, the sun 500, 100, 8; and in Greek we find VHS, 400, 8, 200, which becomes IHS in Latin, for the Greek Upsilon changes to Y and I in Latin, and so we obtain the anagram of "Iesus hominum Salvator."

Kircher points out a Greek example of magic squares; the names Jesus and Mary, and IESOUS MARIA have a curious relation. Iesous is 10, 8, 200, 70, 400, 200 = 888. Now take Maria, 40, 1, 100, 10, 1 = 152. Set 152 in a Magic Square of Three, *i.e.*, nine compartments, thus, 1—5—2, 5—2—1, 2—1—5, then the totals are all 888. The letters of Iesous also make a magic square of 36 divisions, adding every way to 888. Consult the "Arithmologia" of Kircher.

Remember "*illius meminit Sybilla de nomina ejus vaticinando,*" "*onoma Sou monades, dekades, ekaton tades okto,*" or "*nomen tuum 8 unitates, 8 denarii, 8 centenarii.*"—See St. Augustine, *De Civitate Dei.*

Note the mystic word Abraxas is 1, 2, 100, 1, 60, 1, 200 = 365 in Greek letters.

As a curiosity, note that the Roman X for 10 is two V's, which are each 5; C, or, squarely drawn, L, for 100 consists of two L's which are each 50. Priscian says I for 1 was taken from i in the middle of the Greek *mia*, female of *eis*, 1, and V for 5 because it was the fifth vowel. To remember Hebrew numerals note A, I, Q = 1, 10, 100; and in Greek A, I, R, A= 1, 10, 100, 1,000.

According to "The Canon," of 1897, an anonymous work, a Vesica piscis (the figure formed by the intersection of two equal circles) whose dimensions are 26 and 15, is a symbol of the hidden rule or canon by which Natural laws were represented to Initiates in the secret wisdom of the Ancient Mysteries. The Greek gods Zeus, Jupiter and Apollo, the Sun god, have the same numerical relation.

PART IV. THE INDIVIDUAL NUMERALS

THE MONAD. 1

THE number One or the Monad has been defined by the mathematician Theon of Smyrna as "the principal and element of numbers, which while multitute can be lessened by subtraction, is itself deprived of every number and remains stable and firm"; hence as number it is indivisible, it remains immutable, and even multiplied into itself remains itself only, since once one is still one, and the monad multiplied by the monad remains the immutable monad to infinity. It remains by itself among numbers, for no number can be taken from it, or separated from its unity. Proclus observed: "The first monad is the world itself; the second is the inerratic sphere; then thirdly succeed the spheres of the planets, each a unity; then lastly are the spheres of the elements which are also Monads"; and these as they have a perpetual subsistence are called wholenesses—*holotetes* in Greek.

The Monad, Unity, or the number One received very numerous meanings. Photius tells us that the Pythagoreans gave it the following names:—

1. God, the First of all things, the maker of all things.

2. Intellect, the source of all ideas.

3. Male and Female—both together produce all things; from the odd proceed both odd and even.

4. Matter, the last development of universality.

5. Chaos, which resembles the infinite, indifferentiation.

6. Confusion. 7. Commixion. 8. Obscurity, because in the Ineffable principle of things, of which it is the image, all is confused, vague and in darkness.

9. A Chasm, as a void.

10. Tartarus, from its being at the lowest extremity, is dissimilarly similar to God, at the highest end of the series.

11. The Styx, from its immutable nature.

12. Horror, the ineffable, is perfectly unknown and is therefore terrible.

13. Void of Mixture, from the simplicity of the nature of the ineffable.

14. Lethe, oblivion, ignorance.

15. A Virgin, from the purity of its nature.

16. Atlas, it connects, supports, and separates all things.

17. The Sun. 18. Apollo. 19. Pyralios, dweller in fire. 20. Morpho. 21. The Axis. 22. Vesta, or the fire in the centre of the earth. 23. Spermatic Reason. 24. "The point within a circle," "the Central Fire Deity."

The lingam, an upright pillar, was its Hindoo symbol.

The Monad being esteemed the Father of numbers is the reason for the universal prejudice in favour of Odd Numbers over Even ones, which are but copies of the first even number the Dyad, or universal Mother; the father being more esteemed than the mother, for "Might."

Odd numbers were given to the greater Gods, and even ones to the inferior and terrestrial deities.

The number one is represented in the Roman and Arabic systems, by an upright simple line, but in many old systems whose numerals were their letters, we find that almost universally the letter A, from being chosen to commence the set of letters, had the task of representing the Monad.

In Numeration, note that the Romans began with lines, I, II, III, IIII, and then followed the Acute Angle V for 5, then for ten this was doubled X, for fifty the angle was laid down and became L, for a hundred, two fifties, one inverted became C, for five hundred C and L became D.

Hermias, the Christian philosopher, author of "Ridicule of the Gentile Philosophers," quotes from the Pythagoreans; "The Monad is the Beginning of all things"—"*arche ton panton he monas.*"

The figure of one signifies identity, equality, existence and preservation, it signifies living man" alone among animals "erect"; on adding a head we make of it P, the sign of creative Power (paternity, phallus, Pan, the Greek gods and Priapus, all commencing with the vocable P).

Another dash added, and we have man walking, advancing, with foot set forward, in the letter R, which signifies "fens," "iturus," or "advancing."

Compare Unity, *solus*, alone, the unique principle of good; with *Sol*, Sun God, the emblem of supreme power; and they are identical.

The Hebrew word for One is AChD, achad, and it is often put for God; God's One voice to man is the *Bath Kol*, the echo or daughter of the Divine Voice.

The Talmud in Berachoth vi. 1 says that the Shekinah shall rest even upon One who studies the Law. One pang of remorse is of more avail for reformation than many stripes.

One thing obtained with difficulty is more valued than a hundred obtained with ease. Talmud.

It is indiscreet for one man to sleep in a house alone, for fear that he may be attacked by Lilith, who was said to have been Adam's first wife; she is the Night Spectre, and has also power over newly-born infants who are not protected by an Amulet.

Rabbi Nathan exhorted—"Repent One day before thy death"; a wise maxim inculcating the duty of being ever prepared; every day some advance in knowledge and goodness should be attained.

Ever work and ever pray, "for the road winds upward all the way," as the Lord Buddha taught in ancient India.

THE DYAD. 2

As was the case with the Monad so the Dyad also was said to represent a large number of different objects and ideas; things indeed so dissimilar that it is difficult to understand how such multiplicity of opinion arose.

And first it is the general opposite to the Monad, the cause of dissimilitude, the interval between multitude and the Monad. Of figures, those which are characterised by equality and sameness have relation to the Monad; but those in which inequality and difference predominate are allied to the Dyad. Monad and Dyad are also called Bound and Infinity.

1. It was called "Audacity," from its being the earliest number to separate itself from the Divine One; from the "Adytum of God-nourished Silence," as the Chaldean oracles say.

2. It was called "Matter" as being definite and the cause of bulk and division.

3. It is called "the interval between Multitude and the Monad," because it is not yet perfect multitude, but is parturient with it. Of this we see an image in the Dyad of Arithmetic, for, as Proclus observes, "The dyad is the medium between unity and number, for unity by addition produces more than by multiplication, but number by addition produces less than by multiplication; whilst the Dyad, whether added to itself or multiplied by itself, produces the same."

4. "Fountain of Symphony," and "Harmony."

5. Erato, because it attracts the Monad, like Love, and another number is formed.

6. Patience, because it is the first number that endures separation from the Monad.

7. Phanes, or Intelligible Intellect.

8. It is the fountain of all Female divinities, and hence Nature, Rhea and Isis.

9. Cupid, just as Erato, from desiring its opposite for a partner.

In Astronomy, we speak of 2 nodes, Caput and Cauda Draconis; and in Astrology of 2 aspects of the planets, Benefic and Malefic.

The Two Pillars IKIN and BOZ at the entrance of King Solomon's Temple are notable symbols of Strength and Stability; they are comparable to the Two Beings, Kratos and Bia, who appear in the Play by Æschylus, as a male and a female potency, who bind Prometheus.

The Chinese speak of Blue as the colour of Heaven, because made up of Red, Male, and Black, Female; of the active and the passive; the brilliant and the obscure.

The followers of Pythagoras spoke of two kinds of enjoyment. First, lasciviousness and indulgence of the belly, like the murderous songs of Sirens; second, honest and just indulgences, which bring on no repentance.

Hierocles says 2 things are necessary to life, the aid of kindred, and benevolent sympathy of one's neighbours.

A notable ancient Egyptian hieroglyphic was formed of two serpents in connection with a globe or egg, representing the world. Another celebrated pair, in connection with worship, is the association of a tree and a serpent, referring as some say to the Mosaic account of the Tree of Knowledge and the Tempter Serpent. Some have supposed that it is only since the condemnation "on thy Belly shalt thou go" that the Serpent has been limbless, and obliged to crawl.

Note, it has been argued, and by a great churchman too, that the whole tale rests on error, and that for serpent we should read "Ape" (Rev. Adam Clarke). This is substituting one error for another.

In the orgies of Bacchus Mænades, the worshippers had snakes twined in their hair and danced, singing "Eve, Eve, by whom came the sin." See Clemens Alexandrinus, Protrept. 9.

Duality introduces us to the fatal alternative to Unity or Good, namely EVIL; and to many other human and natural contrasts—night and day, light and darkness, wet and dry, hot and cold, health and disease, truth and error, male and female, which man having fallen from his high estate, from spirit to matter, cannot avoid associating himself with. Two is a number of Mourning and Death, misfortunes are apt to follow; turn to our History of England, see the unhappiness of Kings numbered the second of each name—William II., Edward II., and Richard II. of England were all murdered.

The Romans dedicated the 2nd month to Pluto, God of Hades, and on the 2nd day of it they offered sacrifices to the Manes.

Pope John XIX. instituted the Fête des Trépassés (All Souls' Day) on November 2nd, the second month of Autumn.

The Two Talmuds of the Jews, among other quaint notions, have the following ideas of the number Two.

It is not every man who deserves to have two tables; this meant that very few deserve to have the best of the next life, as well as the good things of this one.

There are two important things; first, that one's bed should be placed north to south, and that one should pray in front of his bed. There are two ways before a man, one leads to Paradise and one to Gai-hinnom, the place of punishment.

There are only two Jewish laws, the written law of Moses, and the oral law of the Kabalah.

Every Jew who goes from the Synagogue to his house on the eve of the Sabbath is accompanied by two angels, one good and one bad, and if the house is all in order the good angel confirms a blessing, but if it be in disorder the good angel has to say Amen to the condemnation spoken by the evil angel.

Two are better than three; this means youth is better than old age with its staff of support.

There were two women notorious for their pride, and their names were contemptible; Deborah meant *wasp*, and Hulda *weasel*. Many persons nowadays believe that birth names somehow affect their owners, as names given are prophetic of the nature and fate of the person.

Speech may be worth one Selah (a Jewish coin), but silence is worth Two.

A certain man had two wives, one young and one old; when he was forty and inclined to become grey, the young one pulled out all the grey hairs, and the old wife pulled out all his black hairs; so he became bald. Which things point a moral as well as adorn a tale.

Given two dry firebrands of wood and one of green, the dry will destroy the green.

Two dogs once killed a lion, so the minority must at last always give way to a majority.

The Talmud argues that Adam had two faces; some say one before and one behind, while others say one looked to right and one to the left. Others say that Adam was both a male and a female. Others say that Eve was made from his thirteenth rib, and was not drawn out from his head, lest she should be vain; not from his eyes, lest she should be wanton; not from his mouth, lest she should talk too much; not from his ears, lest she should be an eavesdropper; not from his feet, lest she should be a gadabout; and not from his heart, lest she should be jealous: yet in spite of all these precautions woman has developed all these faults.

Of two who quarrel, he or she who first gives in shows the noblest nature.

Two negatives or affirmatives are as good as an oath. Shevuoth, 36, 1.

The Twos of the Two Testaments are two Tables of the Law; the Disciples were sent out two and two; two disciples were sent by Jesus to fetch the ass's colt; two to make ready the Passover; two disciples buried Jesus; Caleb and Joshua were the two spies; two angels rescued Lot; there were two witnesses of the Resurrection, and two of the Ascension.

The Book of Revelation of St. John the Divine speaks of Two Witnesses, two olive trees and two candlesticks.

If a dream was dreamed two times it foretold a truth; as in Genesis xli., Judges vi., First Book of Kings, chapters ix. and xi.

The animal kingdom shows all sexual generation to arise from pairs of contrasted beings, the male and female; the microscope now discovers to us the spermatozoon and the ovum, but the truth was known of old to philosophers of India, Egypt and the Gnostics, in whose lore we find human generation to spring from the Serpent and the Egg.

THE TRIAD. 3

PHOTIUS observes that the Triad is the first odd number in energy, is the first perfect number, and is a middle and analogy.

The Pythagoreans referred it to Physiology; it is the cause of all that has the triple dimension.

It is also the cause of good counsel, intelligence, and knowledge, and is a Mistress of Music, mistress also of Geometry, possesses authority in whatever pertains to Astronomy and the nature and knowledge of the heavenly bodies, connects and leads them into effects.

Every virtue also is suspended from it, and proceeds from it.

In Mythology it is referred by Nicomachus to:

1. Saturn, Time, past, present, and future. 2. Latona. 3. The Horn of Amalthea, the nurse of Jupiter. 4. Polyhymnia, among the Muses.

Number being more increased by multiplication than it is by addition, the number 3 is, properly speaking, the first number, as neither the Dyad nor Monad are so increased.

It is a "Middle and Analogy," because all comparisons consist of three terms, at least; and analogies were called by the ancients "middles."

It was considered the Mistress of Geometry because the triangle is the principal of Figures.

With. regard to the Heavenly bodies, the number Three is important; there are 3 quaternions of the celestial signs, the fixed, the movable, and the common.

In every Zodiacal sign also there are 3 faces, and 3 decans, and 3 Lords of their Triplicity; and among the planets there are 3 Fortunes and 3 Infortunes; according to the Chaldeans also, there are 3 Ethereal words prior to the sphere of our Fixed Stars.

On account of the perfection of the Triad, oracles were delivered from a Tripod, as is related of the Oracle at Delphi.

With regard to Music, 3 is said to be Mistress, because Harmony contains 3 symphonies, the Diapason, the Diapente, and the Diatessaron.

Ezekiel xiv. v. 14 mentions 3 men who saw a creation, destruction, and a restoration; Noah of the whole world, Daniel of the Jewish world Jerusalem, and Job of his. personal world.

Note the Hindoo Trinity of Brahma, who consists of Brahma, Vishnu, and Siva; Creator, Preserver, and Changer: in India each has still a special sect of worshippers, who mark themselves with particular emblems; the Vaishnavas are much the most numerous.

The living were of old called "the 3 times blessed" (the dead 4 times blessed).

There were Three cities of Refuge on the East side of the Jordan: Bezer, Ramoth Gilead, and Gozan; and Three on the West: Hebron, Shechem, and Kedesh Naphtali.

Three Fates: Clotho, Lachesis, Atropos.

„ Furies: Tisiphone, Alecto, Megæra.

„ Graces: Euphrosyne, Aglaia, Thalia, says Hesiod.

„ Judges of Hades: Minos, Æacus, Rhadamanthus.

„ Horæ: Hesiod says they were Eunomia (Order), Dike (Justice), Eirene (Peace).

Jupiter's thunder is "triformis." Hecate is always called "triple."

Neptune's spear is a trident, and so has Siva the Trisula.

Pluto's dog Cerberus had 3 heads.

There were Three founders of the Roman Empire: Romulus, B.C. 753, Camillus, B.C. 389, expelled the Gauls; and Caius Marius, B.C. 102, who overthrew the hordes of Cambrians and Teutons.

The Jewish Rabbis say that the Sword of Death has 3 drops of Gall, one drops in the mouth and the man dies, from the second comes the pallor of death, and the third turns the carcase to dust. See Purchas, "The Pilgrimage," 1613.

A letter Yod within an equilateral triangle was a symbol of the ineffable name Jehovah and was so used by the Jews. The moderns have pointed out that this form suggests the idea that they knew something of a Triune God. Other monograms of Jehovah were also triple; thus 3 rays, and the Shin, and three yods in a triangle.

Under the number 3 also we may in passing mention the Royal Arch sign, the "Triple Tau," three T's united: the manner of its explanation, and the ideas which it represents, are not fit matters for description in his work. Note also 3 stones of the arch, 3 Principals and 3 Sojourners; 3 Veils; and in the Craft Lodges, 3 officers, 3 degrees, 3 perambulations.

In the Roman Cultus, the number 3 is of constant occurrence, as for example see Virgil, Eclogue 8, The Pharmaceutria; the priests used a cord of 3 coloured strands, and an image was carried 3 times round an altar.

"Terna tibi hæc primum triplici diversa colore."

The Druids also paid a constant respect to this number; and even their poems are noted as being composed in Triads. It is not necessary here to enlarge upon the transcendent importance of the Christian Trinity. In old paintings we often see a Trinity of Jesus with John and Mary.

In the "Timæus" of Plato, the Divine Triad is called Theos—God, Logos—The Word, and Psyche—the Soul. Indeed it is impossible to study any single system of worship throughout the world, without being struck by the peculiar persistence of the triple number in regard to divinity; whether as a group of deities, a triformed or 3-headed god, a Mysterious Triunity, a deity of 3 powers, or a family relationship of 3 Persons, such as the Father, Mother and Son of the Egyptians, Osiris, Isis and Horus.

And again in the various faiths we see the chief Dignity given in turn to each person of the Triad: some rejoice in the patriarchal Unity, some in the greater glory of the Son, and others again lavish all their adoration on the Great Mother; even in trinities of coequal males, each has his own special worshippers; note this especially among the Hindoos, where for example the followers of Vishnu are called Vaishnavas: to complicate matters too, in this case each deity has his female potency or sakti, and these also have their own adherents.

Under this notice of the Triad we may refer to the emblem of the Isle of Man, three legs united at the hips; this is supposed to have been derived from Sicilian Mariners at an early date, for the same emblem is found at Palermo in Sicily, and this design is there to be seen on an old public building. Sicily was anciently named Trinacria, from its three promontories.

Three is a notable number in the mythology of the Norseman: the great Ash-tree Yggdrasil supported the world; it had three roots; one extended into Asgard, the abode of the Gods; one into Jotenheim, the home of the Giants, and the third into Nifleheim, the region of the Unknown. The three Norns (Fates) attend to the root in Asgard: they were Urda—the past; Verdandi—the present; and Skulda—the future.

The Talmuds are crowded with quaint conceits concerning the Triad, and many are very curious.

The ancient Hebrews said there are three night watches, in the first the ass brays, in the second the dog barks, in the third the mother suckles her infant and converses with her husband.

He who three times daily repeats the 114th Psalm is sure of future happiness.

Three precious gifts were given to the Jews; the Law of Moses, the Land of Israel, and Paradise.

In three sorts of dreams there is truth; the last dream of the morning, the dream which is also dreamed by a neighbour, and a dream twice repeated.

Three things calm a man; melody, scenery and sweet scent: and three things improve a man; a fine house, a handsome wife, and good furniture.

He who is born on the Third day of the week will be rich and amorous.

Three despise their fellows; cooks, fortune-tellers and dogs.

Three love their fellows; proselytes, slaves and ravens.

Three persons live a life which is no life; he who lives at another man's table, he who is ruled by his wife, and he who is incapable from bodily affliction.

Orthodox Jews were very particular about the cuttings from the nails; a pious man buries them, an orderly man burns them, but he who throws them away is wicked; for if a woman step over them, mischance may follow. Moed Katon, 18. 1. The nails should be trimmed on a Friday and never on a Thursday.

There are three keys which God keeps to himself, and which no man can gain nor use; the key of life, the key of rain and the key of the resuscitation of the dead. Taanith, 2; 1 and 2.

The Jewish butcher of Kosher meat must use three knives; one to slaughter the animal, another to cut it up, and a third to remove the suet which was unlawful food; as pork is.

Three acolytes must attend the High Priest when he went in to worship; one at his right, one at his left, and one had to hold up the gems on the train of his vestment.

There are three parts of a man. The father gives the white parts, bones, nails, brain and the whites of the eyes; the mother gives the red parts, skin, flesh, etc.: while God gives the breath, soul, mind and senses.

The Sanhedrim could order as a punishment three degrees of Excommunication—separation for an undefined time, exclusion for 60 days, and execration for 30 days. Moed Katon, 17. 1.

The name of Adam is of three letters, A, D and M: these are the initials of Adam, David and Messiah, and the Soul of the first passed to David and then to the Messiah. Nishmath Chajim, 152. 2.

The Soul of Cain passed to Jethro, his spirit into Korah, and his body to an Egyptian. Yalkut Reuben, 9. 18. 24.

The Soul of Eve passed to Sarah, to Hannah the Shunamite, and then to the widow of Zarepta. The Soul of Rahab passed to Heber the Kenite. The Soul of Jael passed to Eli. Some Souls of pious Jews pass into the persons of the Gentiles, so that they shall plead for Israel. Some evil Hebrew souls have passed into animals, as that of Ishmael into the she-ass of Balaam, and later into the ass of Rabbi Pinchas ben Yair. The Soul of a slanderer may be transmigrated into a stone, so as to become silent; and the Soul of a murderer into water. Emeh Hemelech, 153. 1. 2.

There are three causes of dropsy, depending on diseases of the breast, the liver and the kidneys.

There are three forms of coma, that is insensibility; due to brain injury, brain disease and brain poisoning.

There are three modes of death, beginning either at the brain, the lungs or the heart. Bichat, Physiologie.

One Zodiacal Sign, that of Scorpio, has three emblems; the eagle in the highest symbolism, the snake, and the scorpion in evil aspects only.

Astrologic Natal Figures are often erroneous by reason of the alleged moment of birth being incorrect: there are three modes of Rectification, two are ancient, the Animodar of Ptolemy and the Trutine of Hermes; and there is one modern method, the Natal Epoch of W. R. Old.

In both the Old and the New Testaments we find the Day was divided into three day watches and four night watches. The mediæval occultists divided the days into Planetary hours, the scheme of alternation occupied a week, 7 days × 24 hours= 168 hours, so 168 hours are divisible among the Seven Planets, each day beginning with its own different one; see Harleian MSS. 6483, and "The Herbal," Culpepper, 1814.

There is also another scheme in which the planets are related to a six-hour period by Ragon and Blavatsky.

Among the Brahmins there were three great Vedas; three Margas or ways of salvation; three Gunas, the Satva, quiescence; Rajas, desire; and Tamas, decay. Three Lokas, Swarga, Bhumi and Patala; heaven, earth and hell. Three Jewels of wisdom, the Tri-ratnas; Buddha, Dharma and Sanga. The three Fires being the three aspects of the human soul, Atma, Buddhi and Manas. There were three prongs of the trident, and three eyes in the forehead of Siva. Note also the 3-syllabled Holy Word AUM.

At the Oblation of the Elements in the Celtic Church, 3 drops of Wine and 3 drops of water were poured into the chalice. In the present Christian Church we notice 3 crossings with water at Baptism, 3 Creeds; the Banns of Marriage are published 3 times; and a Bishop in benediction makes the sign of the Cross 3 times.

In Roman Catholic churches, the Angelus Bell is rung three times a day, a peal of 3 times 3 for the heavenly hierarchies of angels: Pope John XXII. ordered that the faithful should say 3 *Aves* on each occasion.

In civil life the usher of a court 3 times repeats the warning Oyez, Oyez, Oyez, which word means "hear" or "listen."

Note also the emblem of the Irish nation, the Shamrock, which has a three-lobed leaf, the *Oxalis acefosella*.

The Trigrams of Fo-hi should be studied in "The Yi-King," a book of Ancient China said to have been the production of King Wan and his son, Kau. The great Confucius wrote a supplement to it. This book is a mystical work on Symbolism referring to Cosmogony, to Man, and to the purposes of life. The initial symbols are the Yang, male, and the Yin, female. Then follow 8 trigrams, formed of emblematical lines; they are:—khien, tui, li, chan, sien, khan, kan and kwan; each expressed by figures of one long and two short lines. Some say that one Fo-Hi invented these symbols. A later Mystic expanded the system into 64 figures, each composed of 6 lines of whole and half lines. With these were associated two diagrams formed of circles, named the "River Horse," and the "Writing of Lo": these will repay the contemplation of modern occultists. Yang, male, is also associated with Heaven, the Sun, Light and 25 the total of the odd units. Yin, female, with the Moon, the Earth, darkness and the number 30, the total of the even numbers to ten. See "Sacred Books of the East"; "The Yi-King."

THREE AND A HALF. 3½.

W. F. SHAW calls attention to the number 3½ as being of mystical importance, as the half of seven, typifying present suffering as compared with future joy. The famine in the time of Elias, when Israel was persecuted by Ahab and Jezebel, lasted 3½ years. Antiochus Epiphanes persecuted the church 3½ years. Forty-two months, or 3½ years, are symbolical of times of trouble. Jesus preached 3½ years.

In the Revelations, the Bride, the Lamb's Wife, suffers 1260 days in the wilderness, being a time, times, and a half, Rev. xii. 6–14. Again the Holy City is said to be trodden under foot forty-two months, or 3½ years. The two witnesses testify 3½ years, and their dead bodies remain unburied 3½ days: so also the scattering of the holy people as mentioned in Daniel xii. 7 is for three times and a half, by which we were to understand a period of suffering.

THE TETRAD. 4.

THE Pythagoreans, said Nicomachus, call the number four "the greatest miracle," "a God after another manner," "a manifold divinity," the "fountain of Nature," and its "key bearer." It is the "introducer and cause of the permanency of the Mathematical discipline." It is "most masculine" and "robust"; it is Hercules and Æolus. It is Mercury, Vulcan, and Bacchus. Among the Muses, Urania. They also called it Feminine, effective of Virility, and an Exciter of Bacchic fury. In harmony, it was said to form by the quadruple ratio the symphony dis-diapason. They called it Justice, as the first evenly even number.

As a type of Deity, we all know of the famous Hebrew title Tetra-grammaton or unpronounceable name we call Jehovah IHVH: this Name was used by the Kabalistic Rabbis to hide their secret tenets of the Divine Essence of the Creator God.

Almost all the peoples of Antiquity possessed a name for Deity consisting of four letters, and many of them considered 4 to be a Divine number, thus:—

In Hebrew we find also IHIH called Eheie; and AHIH called Aheie.

Assyrian ADAD, Egyptian AMUN, Persians SYRE or SIRE, Greek ThEos, Latin DEUS, German GOTT, French DIEU, Turkish ESAR, Tartar ITGA, Arabian ALLH, Allah, Samaritan JABE, Egyptian TEUT, TAUT, THOTh.

In Sanchoniathon we find the Deity called IEVO.

In Clemens Alexandrinus „ „ „ JAOU.

Attention should be paid to the Sanscrit holy phrase, aspiration or prayer of Four syllables— "Aum mani padme hum"—literally, "Oh, the Jewel in the Lotus" (meaning "the Divine spark within man").

Theon of Smyrna, in the edition of Ismael Bullialdo, 1644, page 147, says, "The Tetractys was not only principally honoured by the Pythagoreans because all symphonies exist within it, but also because it appears to contain the nature of all things," hence their oath, "Not by him who delivered to our souls the Tetractys" (that is Pythagoras), this tetractys is seen in the COMPOSITION of the first numbers 1. 2. 3. 4.

But the 2nd Tetractys arises from the increase by MULTIPLICATION of odd and even numbers beginning from the Monad.

The 3rd subsists according to Magnitude.

The 4th is in simple Bodies, Monad-Fire, Dyad-Air, Triad-Water, Tetrad-Earth.

The 5th is of the figures of Bodies, Pyramid-Fire, Octahedron-Air, Icosahedron-Water, Cube-Earth.

The 6th of Vegetative Life, Seed-Monad or point; if it increase in length—dyad-line; in breadth—triad-superficies; in thickness—tetrad-solid.

The 7th is of Communities; as Man, House, Street, City.

The 8th is the Judicial power: Intellect, Science, Opinion, Sense.

The 9th is of the parts of the Animal, the Rational, Irascible and Epithymetic soul, and the Body they live in.

The 10th Tetractys is of the Seasons of the Year, spring, summer, autumn, winter.

The 11th Tetractys is of the Ages of Man, the infant, the lad, the man, and the senex.

And all are proportional one to another, and hence they said "all things are assimilated to number."

They also gave a four-fold distribution of goods to the Soul and Body, to the Soul, Prudence, Temperance, Fortitude, Justice; and to the Body, Acuteness of senses, Health, Strength, Beauty.

The Objects of desire are 4: viz., Prosperity, Renown, Power, Friendship.

The celebrated 4 Causes of Aristotle may be mentioned here:

Divinity as the cause—by which; υπ' ου up ou.

Matter—from which; εξ ου ex ou.

Form—through which; δι ου di΄ ou.

Effect with reference to which; προς ου pros ou.

The Dead also are called 4 times Blessed; and the Living but thrice blessed.

The number 4 being the completion of the quaternary group of point, line, superficies and body, has also this character that its elements 1, 2, 3, and 4 when summed up are equal to 1 0, which is so perfect that we can go no further, but to increase we must return to the Monad.

It was also called Kosmos, the World, because it formed the number 36, when its digits were thus combined:

$1 + 2 = 3$

$3 + 4 = 7$

$5 + 6 = 11$

$7 + 8 = 15$

$$\overline{36}$$

being the sum of the first four odd numbers with the first

four even numbers.

Plutarch, "De Anim. Procr." 1027, says the world consists of a double Quaternary; 4 of the intellectual World, T'Agathon, Nous, Psyche and Hyle; that is Supreme Wisdom or Goodness, Mind, Soul, Matter, and four of the Sensible World, forming the Kosmos of Elements, Fire, Air, Earth and Water; pur, aer, gē and πυρ, αηρ, γη, υδωρ.

Four is the number of the moons or satellites of Jupiter and Uranus.

The Arabians analysed Female Beauty into nine fours; as:

Four Black—Hair, eyebrows, eyelashes, eyes.

Four White—Skin, white of the eyes, teeth, legs.

Four Red—Tongue, lips, cheeks, gums.

Four Round—Head, neck, forearms, ancles.

Four Long—Back, fingers, arms, legs.

Four Wide—Forehead, eyes, seat, lips.

Four Fine—Eyebrows, nose, lips, fingers.

Four Thick—Buttocks, thighs, calves, knees.

Four Small—Breasts, ears, hands, feet.

See Lane's edition of the "Arabian Nights."

In the Rosicrucian writings of Behmen, Fludd and Maier, we find the occult dogma that the four elements are peopled by spirits, beings who may have influence on the destiny of Man; thus the Earth was inhabited by Gnomes; the Air was inhabited by Sylphs; the Fire was inhabited by Salamanders; and the Water by Undines; these are now commonly called "Elementals." See "Lives of the Necromancers," W. Godwin; Michael Maier; Jacob Behmen's Works.

The existence of Elementals, scoffed at by modern education, is really suggested in a large number of places in both Old and New Testaments, the inspired volume of the Christians: examine, for example, Judges ix. 23; 1 Samuel xvi. 14; Psalm lxxviii. 49; Acts xvi. 16, xix. 13, xxvii. 23; Ephesians vi. 12, ii. 2.

But above all consider the meaning of the Canticle "Benedicite omnia opera" in the book of Common Prayer, "O ye stars, O ye showers and dew, O ye fire and heat, O ye winds, O ye green things, O ye mountains and hills, bless ye the Lord, praise him and magnify him for ever." These phrases are either folly, or else they recognise the spiritual essences or beings inherent in the elements and created things. Again, read hymn 269 in Hymns Ancient and Modern, a most orthodox volume. "Principalities and powers, watch for thy unguarded hours," and Hymn 91, "Christian, dost thou see them, on the holy ground, How the troops of Midian compass thee around?" If these are not the evil elementals, what are they?

Francis Barrett mentions the 4 Consecrated Animals, Lion, Eagle, Man and Calf, emblems of the Kerubim on the terrestrial plane; 4 Archangels, Michael, Gabriel, Uriel, Raphael; note, all end in the Deity name, el, *i.e.* AL, of the Hebrews.

The Gnostics said that all their edifice rested on a 4-pillared Basis; Truth, Intelligence, Silence, Bathos.

Note the earth was formed on the 4th day, according to the allegory found in the Jewish "Genesis," and is the 4th world in a chain of spheres, say the Hindoos.

The figure of 4, as Ragon remarks, is the upright man, carrying the triangle or Divinity, a type of the Trinity of Godhead.

On the Hebrew Magical word AGLA, see the chapter on the Kabalah, page 27.

Note 4 elements, 4 sides of a square and 4 angles;

4 qualities, cold, hot, dry, damp, 4 humours;

4 seasons of the year; 4 quarters of the horizon;

4 Rivers of Eden; Euphrates, Gihon, Hiddekel and Pison;

4 Rivers of the Infernal Regions according to the Greeks, Phlegethon, Cocytus, Styx and Acheron;

4 elements of Metaphysics; Being, essence, virtue, action.

4 Masonic virtues.

4 Evangelists and Gospels; Matthew, Mark, Luke, John, related to the Four Kerubic forms of the Man, Lion, Bull and Eagle, and thus to the Zodiacal Signs—Aquarius, Leo, Taurus and Scorpio (the relation of Aquila to Scorpio is a Rosicrucian secret).

One of the abstruse dogmas of the Kabalah concerns the Four Worlds of Emanation; Atziluth, Briah, Yetzirah and Assiah; these are not worlds in any ordinary sense, but rather planes of development and existence, the former most diaphanous and exalted, the others becoming more and more concrete and manifest; the ten Sephiroth exist on each plane, those of the higher planes being more sublime than those of the lowest; each world has a secret name and number.

Man displays 4 evil tendencies, one in opposition to each of these 4 Worlds; an evil inclination, evil thoughts, evil words, and evil actions. (Isaac Myer.)

Vulcan gave Apollo and Diana arrows on the 4th day of their Nativity: this, says Sir Thomas Browne, is the Gentile equivalent to the Creation of the Sun and Moon on the 4th day.

The Talmud lays down the law as to a woman's drinking, saying one cup of wine is good for her, two do her harm, three demoralize her, and the fourth converts her into a female animal. There are 4 persons who are little better than dead; the blind, the leper, the pauper and he who has no sons.

There are 4 sorts of passionate men; he who is easily provoked and is as easily pacified, he loses more than he gains; he who is not readily provoked and is difficult to appease, he gains more than he loses; the pious man, who is not easily provoked but is easily pacified; and he who is easily provoked and is with difficulty appeased, he is a wicked man.

There are 4 sorts of pupils in occult science; he who learns and then will not teach; he who wants to teach and does not learn; he who learns and then teaches; and lastly, he who listens and won't learn and can't teach.

Four things deter a man from sin: the thought of whence he comes, the fear of where he may go, the conception of who his judge will be, and what his fate may be at the Judgment.

Four persons should offer up thank offerings; he who returns safe from a sea voyage, he who has safely crossed a desert, he who has recovered from an illness, and he who is released from prison. These are referred to in Psalm cvii.

Four men have died from original sin, the work of the Serpent, for they themselves did no ill; Benjamin, Amram the father of Moses, Jesse the father of David, and Chilah the son of David. Sabbat. 55. 2.

At the end of the Passion Fast every Hebrew should drink 4 glasses of wine, even if the price robs him of other necessaries.

The Talmud says that only 4 men had entered Paradise (Pardes, the Garden of Holiness); this meant the state of supernal communion with God, the Beatific Vision, by profound abstraction of mind. These were the Rabbis Ben Azai, Ben Zoma, Asher and Akiba.

The tractate Yoma says God will pardon a man three times for a sin, but the fourth occasion is fatal.

The Jewish Sanhedrin had power to order 4 sorts of death penalty; by stoning, beheading, burning and strangling. The Sanhedrin as a Court of Justice ceased with the Second Temple, but the Rabbis taught that if a man incurs the death penalty of either form he still dies in these ways fortuitously, as if he would have been executed by strangling, he will be found to die of drowning or some other form of suffocation. See Sanhedrin, 37. 2.

Job had four entrances to his house, north, south, east and west; so that the poor might enter and find relief from whichever quarter they came.

Four things God repented that he had made; man's evil passions, the Ishmaelites, the Chaldeans and the Captivity.

God has made only 4 women perfect in beauty; Sarah, Abigail, Rahab and Esther; Eve is not included because she was not born of woman. Esther is said to have had golden coloured hair.

Of the 4 Cardinal points, God left the North Pole unfinished, saying, "if there be any my equal let him finish it like the others." This corner is the home of demons, ghosts, devils and storms. Pirke of Rabbi Eleazar, cap. 3.

The number 4 is related to Jacob, the Lesser Light, which is the Moon. Jacob was spelled IOQB, and its initials are those of epithets IUTzR the Former; OUShU the Maker, QUNA the Possessor, and BVRA, the Creator. See Amos vii. 2, where Jacob is called the "small."

In Christian dogma, Christ the triple deity on the Cross of 4 limbs, is the descent of Spirit into Matter: or, as the Theosophists say, the Triad of "Atma-Buddhi-Manas descends into the Quaternary of personal Man, the Kama, Prana, Linga and Sthula Sarira."

The 4 Cabeiri, or great deities of Syro-Phenicia, were Axieros, Axiokersos, Axiokersa and Kasmillos, children of Sydyk, are named by Sanchoniathon and quoted by Eusebius.

In the ancient Egyptian form of burial, while the body was made into a swathed mummy, the internal organs of the chest and abdomen were removed and preserved in 4 jars, often called the Canopic Jars; they were dedicated to the 4 Genii of the Cardinal points, who were at times called the Children of Horus. The jar of Amset, Amesheth or Mestha, the South, was man-shaped, and in it were put the stomach and large intestines; in the jar of Hapi, or Ahephi, the North, dog-headed, were the small intestines; in the jar of Tuamutef or Toumath-path, the East, jackal-headed, were the heart and lungs, and in the jar of Khebsenuf or Kabexnuf, hawk-headed, the West, were the liver and gall bladder. These Vases appear in tombs of the 18th dynasty, and remained in use until the 26th dynasty; according to E. A. Wallis Budge.

These 4 Genii of the dead in Amenti were guarded by 4 Goddesses, viz., by Isis, Nephthys, Neith and Serquet.

The Squares of the Periodic times of the Planets are the Cubes of their mean distance from the Sun.

The Christian Church recognises 4 great Councils, those of Nicæa in A.D. 325; Constantinople, 381; Ephesus, 431; and Chalcedon in 451.

The Western Church recognises 4 great Doctors; St. Ambrose, St. Jerome, St. Augustine, and St. Gregory the Great; and the Eastern Church 4,—St. Athanasius, St. Basil, St. Gregory of Nazianzen, and St. John Chrysostom.

There is a vast fund of mystic lore, known to some Fratres Rosæ Crucis, concerning the Chariot of Ezekiel described in the Mosheh Merkavah or Vision of Ezekiel. The Chagigah of the Talmud says it were better never to have been born than to pry into the 4 sides thereof, what is above and below, before and behind it.

The Ancient Legend of the Four Crowned Martyrs, who were masons, who refused to disclaim their Christian faith and refused to build an idol, has led in our own time to the consecration of the Quatuor Coronati Lodge of Freemasons, which has a corresponding Membership of 3000 brethren: the present author is a Past Master of this Lodge of literary Freemasons.

The "Four Masters" of Ireland of the first half of the 17th century compiled a History of Ireland from B.C. 2242 to A. D. 1616.

Magic Squares were first known by the work of a Greek, Emanuel Moscopulos, still existing in MSS. of the 16th century in the National Library of Paris. Cornelius Agrippa then gave the Planetary Squares, which have been many times copied in subsequent books. From a more mathematical point of view, they have been much studied in France by M. Bachet and M. Frenicle, M. Poignard of Brussels, and de la Hire. M. de la Loubère gives information of the use of Magic Squares by the Indians of Surat.

To the number 4 belong the several forms of the cross, Maltese, Greek, Passional, St. Andrew's and the Fylfot cross—the Swastika. Hermetic philosophy teaches how to view the last as composed from a magic square of 5, giving 25 squares, of which the Fylfot takes 17, referring to the Sun, Signs and Elements. There is a quaint Hebrew association between the name Tetragrammaton, IHVH, the God name, and man formed in his image for if Yod, י: Heh, ה, Vau, ו, Heh, ה be drawn one over the other, the Yod will look like the head above, the Heh will look like the two arms, the Vau will be upright body, and the final Heh will show the two legs.

It is stated in some ancient Persian works that 4 bright stars were placed as guardians at the 4 cardinal points. At the beginning of the Kali Yuga, at Crishna's death at 3102 B.C., the astronomers say that Aldebaran, the eye of Taurus, and Antares, the heart of Scorpio, were as the equinoctial points, and Regulus, the heart of Leo, and Fomalhaut, the eye of the Southern Fish, were near the solstitial points: this was 5003 years ago.

The pack of common playing cards has 4 suits; of diamonds, hearts, clubs and spades; the old Tarot or Tarocchi cards had 4 suits; Wands, Cups, Swords and Pentacles; occult science relates these to the Yod, Heh, Vau, Heh of the Tetragrammaton: the Tarot pack has also 4 Court cards, Cavalier, King, Queen and Violet or Knave; also called Knight, King, Queen and Princess by some mystics.

THE PENTAD. 5.

FROM the Nicomachean Extracts we derive our knowledge of the Pythagorean doctrine of the number five.

It is an eminently spherical and circular number, because in every multiplication it restores itself and is found terminating the number; it is change of Quality, because it changes what has three dimensions into the sameness of a sphere by moving circularly and producing light: and hence "Light" is referred to the number 5.

Also it is the "Privation of Strife," because it unites in friendship the two forms of number even and odd; the 2 and 3. Also Justice from throwing things into the light.

Also the "Unconquered" from a geometrical reason which may be found in Alexander Aphrodisiensis, Commentaries on the 1st Book of Aristotle's Metaphysics.

Also the "Smallest extremity of Vitality," because there are three powers of Life, vegetable, psychical, and rational: and as the Rational is arranged according to the hebdomad, and the Psychical according to the hexad, so the Vegetative power falls under the control of the Pentad.

Proclus on Hesiod gives two reasons for its semblance to Justice, "because it punishes wrong, and takes away inequality of possession, and also equalizes what is less, to benefit."

Also named Nemesis, for it arranges in an appropriate manner all things celestial, divine and natural.

And Venus, because the male 3 triad and the female 2 or dual, odd and even are conjoined in it: Venus was sometimes considered hermaphrodite, and was bearded as well as full-bosomed.

And Gamelia, that is referring to marriage.

And Androgynia, being odd and masculine, yet containing an even female part.

Also a "Demi-goddess," because it is half of the Decad, which is a divinity. And "Didymus," because it divides the Decad into two equal parts. But they called it Pallas, and Immortal, because Pallas presides over the Ether, or 5th Element (akasa) which is indestructible, and is not *material* to our present senses. And Cardiatis or Cordialis, because like a heart it is in the middle of the body of the numbers, thus:—

1	4	7
2	5	8
3	6	9

The ancients had a maxim, "Pass not above the beam of the balance," that is—be not cause of injury; for they said, let the members in a series form a Balance Beam. Thus when a weight depresses the Beam, an obtuse angle is formed by the Depressed side and the Tongue Vertical, and an acute angle on the other. Hence it is worse to do than to suffer injury, and the authors of injury sink down to the infernal regions, but the injured rise to the gods. Since, however, injustice pertains to inequality, equalization is necessary which is effected by addition and subtraction.

Plutarch, in his treatise on the Generation of the Soul according to Plato, states that the Pentad is called "trophos," which equals Sound, because the first of the intervals of a Tone which is capable of producing a sound is the fifth; it is also a type of "Nature."

The Pentalpha or 5-pointed star, an endless complex set of angles, was the emblem of Health, Hygeia; it forms 5 copies of the capital letter A. It is also called the Pentagram, and the Seal of Solomon, and is said to have been the device on the signet-ring of this ancient Grand Master of the Mysteries.

Kenneth Mackenzie remarks that, being formed by the union of the first odd and even numbers, 5 was considered of peculiar value and used as an Amulet or Talisman powerful to preserve from evil, and when inscribed on a portal, could keep out evil spirits; it is found almost everywhere in Greece and Egypt.

Diodorus calls five "the union of the four elements with Ether." There are 5 orders of Architecture; and 5 Senses of the human body now commonly known and described (but the whole are seven). Geometry is technically called the 5th Science. In Masonry the grand scheme is the 5 points of Fellowship, and note also 5 Brethren can hold a Fellowcrafts lodge. It is also called the Pyramid, from the arrangement of Monads, thus three below, then two, then one above them. Note the system of 5 regular Euclidean bodies, tetrahedron, hexahedron or cube, octohedron, dodekahedron and icosahedron.

The Pentagram was the emblem of safety. The Pentacle, the Masons' signet mark (according to Stukeley), was the device borne by Antiochus Soter on a war-banner, to which was ascribed the signal victory he obtained.

The Ancients esteemed this number as a measure for drinking; they mixed 5 parts of water with their wine, and Hippocrates added 1/5 of water to milk as a medical draught.

Phintys, the daughter of Callicrates, describes the Five virtues of a Wife: mental and bodily purity; abstaining from excess of ornament in dress; staying at home; refraining, as females then did, from celebrating public mysteries; piety and temperance.

In Roman marriage ceremonies it was customary to light 5 tapers and to admit the guests by fives; see Plato in Leg. IV.

Theology displays 5 modes of the Conception of God; Pantheism, Polytheism, Dualism, Unitarianism and Trinitarianism.

Jewish references to five are many—5 gifts to the priests, 5 things which might only be eaten in the camp. Not to eat fruit from a tree until it was five years old. The trespass offering imposed on the Philistines, 5 golden emerods and 5 golden mice. Joseph gave Benjamin 5 suits of raiment—Joseph presented only 5 of his brethren to Pharaoh. David took 5 pebbles when he went to fight Goliath.

The Jews classed a Bride's attendants by fives—five wise and five foolish virgins.

There are Five Articles of Belief in the Mahometan faith—in Allah, in Angels, in the prophet, the day of judgment, and predestination.

The Five duties of a Member of the Christian church were stated by the Fathers: To keep holy the festivals; to observe the fasts; to attend public worship; to receive the Sacraments; and to adhere to the customs of the church.

St. Paul said he preferred to speak 5 words in a language understood by his hearers than 10,000 in an unknown tongue.

In arranging an Horoscope some astrologers use only 5 aspects of the planets—the conjunction, the opposition, sextile, trine and square; and the evil or good fortune of the person seems to depend on them.

Among the Romans a display of 5 Wax Candles indicated that a Marriage was being celebrated; and special prayers were also made on such occasions to these 5 deities, Jupiter, Juno, Venus, Pitho, and Diana. See Rabelais, 3. 20.

One of the two main divisions of Flowering Plants is characterised by a predominance of the numbers 4 and 5; these plants have almost a total absence of the numbers 3 and 6 in the component parts of their flowers. These are the Exogens or Dicotyledons; on the other hand the Monocotyledons or Endogens have a constant predominance of the numbers 3 and 6, and a total absence of 4 and 5 symmetry.

There are 5 kinds of intercolumniations in Architecture, mentioned by Vitruvius, determined by the proportions of height and diameter, viz., Pycnostyle, systyle, eustyle, diastyle, and aerostyle.

The Triad Society of China, concerning which we find an article in the *Freemasons' Quarterly Review*, 1845, p. 165, boasts of great antiquity; it resembles Freemasonry in some points: five is a chief mystical number in its concerns. Its seal is pentangular, on its angles are 5 characters representing Too or Saturn, Muh or Jupiter, Shwuv or Mercury, Kin or Venus, and Ho or Mars.

In the Infernal World are 5 terrors and torments; Deadly bitterness, horrible howling, terrible darkness, unquenchable heat and thirst, and a penetrating stench; says old John Heydon, quoting some mediæval father of the Church. He was admitted an Adept among the Fratres Rosæ Crucis, but was never received among the Magistri.

Five styles of architectural columns are described: Tuscan, Doric, Ionic, Corinthian and Composite.

Sir Thomas Browne, 1658, notes an ancient Greek division of vegetables into five classes:—

Sir Thomas Browne

Dendron, Arbor, Tree; Thamnos, Frutex, Bush; Phruganon, Suffrutex, herb; Poa, Herba, grass; and Askion or gymnon, fungus, mushroom and seaweed.

Note the Quintuple section of a Cone—Circle, Ellipse, Parabola, Hyperbola and Triangle. *Agathe tuche*, that is Good fortune, is the old title of Astrologers for the 5th house (succedent) of the Heavens, as shown in an Astrological Figure, and which refers to offspring, success in hazardous schemes of fortune or pleasure, and wealth.

Joshua hanged 5 kings on 5 trees, they were found hidden in a cave, and were the kings of Jerusalem, Hebron, Jarmuth, Lachish and Eglon.

Every important measurement of the Jewish Tabernacle was 5 or a multiple of 5.

The Hebrew letter H, Heh, 5, was in occult Kabalah always deemed of female potency.

There were 5 principal parts of Solomon's Temple.

David Blesses the Lord 5 times in Psalms ciii., civ.

The Talmud says that there are 5 little things which are a terror to 5 strong things; the mosquito to the lion; the gnat to the elephant; the ichneumon fly to the scorpion; the flycatcher bird to the eagle, and the stickleback to the leviathan. Lewisohn, "Zoology of the Talmud."

Five things have in them a one-sixtieth part of 5 other things; fire is one-sixtieth of hell; honey one-sixtieth of manna; the Sabbath one-sixtieth of the Sabbath hereafter; sleep of death; and a dream one-sixtieth of prophecy. Talmud, Berachoth, 57. 2.

Even on the Sabbath you may kill 5 things—the fly in Egypt; the wasp in Nineveh; the scorpion of Hadabia; the serpent of Israel, and the mad dog anywhere. Talmud, Sabbat, 121. 2.

In the First Temple of Solomon were 5 things which were not in the second Temple; the Cherubic Ark; the Shekinah; the Holy Spirit, and the Urim and Thummim. Talmud, Yoma, 21. 2.

Rabies in the dog has 5 symptoms; its mouth gapes; it drops spittle; its ears hang down; it carries its tail between its legs, and it keeps to the side of any path. Yoma, 83. 2.

For suckling mothers there are 5 things which are injurious; garlic, cucumber, melon, leeks and onions: said Rashi.

If one study 5 years and then has found no profit in it; he will never profit by it. Talmud, Chullin, 24. 1.

Five is the number of expiation and of sacrifice, the number of the passions, and the 5 wounds of Christ. These were commemorated anciently by 5 crosses inscribed on the Altar tables, and the Priest made 5 crosses on himself at the canon in the Liturgy. W. F. Shaw.

Jesus 5 times foretold His passion, and gave 5 particulars concerning it, and received 5 wounds.

The Brahmins speak of 5 skandhas, or attributes of men; they are *rupa*, form; *vidana*, perception; *sanina*, consciousness; *sanskara*, action; and *vidyana*, knowledge.

In China 5 means Shangti or Thian, the God in Heaven: the Chinese speak of 5 Blessings—longevity, riches, health, virtue and a natural death.

The ancient Chinese spoke of 5 Elements—earth, wood, fire, metal and water; and of 5 primary colours—yellow, red, white, green and black.

The 5th Element, the Quintessence of the Alchymist, was derivable from the four, by progression—At first the Ens, then the Two Contraries, then the Three Principles, then the Four Elements. Separate the pure from the impure, gently and with judgment, and so you obtain the Quintessence, the Son of the Sun. Similarly note the progression; stone, plant, animal, man, God. The old authors added,—Talia si jungere possis, sit tibi scire satis; to which this Author adds,—sed Quod scis, nescis.

THE HEXAD. 6.

NICOMACHUS calls it "the form of form, the only number adapted to the Soul, the distinct union of the parts of the universe, the fabricator of the Soul, also Harmony," and it is properly "Venus" herself.

It is also Zygeia and Nuptialia, and the Androgynæ who Pliny tells us were an African tribe who had "dextra mamma virilis, læva muliebris." Among the Fates it is Lachesis. Among the Muses it is Thalia.

Six is also Benevolence, Peace, and Health, Acmon, one of the Cyclops (akmon, an anvil), and Truth.

By the Pythagoreans it was called "the Perfection of parts."

As to "Marriage," it is a number equal to its parts, and marriage is a ceremony to sanction the production of offspring similar to the parent.

It is formed by the multiplication of the first (beyond unity) odd number and the first even, it resembles the union of Male and Female, as in Marriage or in Androgyneity, Health and Beauty, on account of its symmetry.

It was called "all-sufficient," παναρκεια, panarkeia.

According to the Pythagoreans, after a period of 216 years, which number is the cube of 6, all things are regenerated, and they said this was the periodic time of the Metempsychosis or the re-birth of man after each death.

When multiplied into itself, like the pentad, six has also always itself in the unit place, thus, 6, 36, 216, 1296, 7776.

On the 6th day Man was created according to Genesis. On the 6th day of the week Jesus died on the cross.

The Israelites had 6 cities of Refuge. Numbers xxxv. v. 6. There were six things hated by Jehovah. Prov. vi. v. 16. The Seraphim of Isaiah had each 6 wings.

In a Freemasons' Lodge there are 6 Jewels, three of which are immovable and lie open in the lodge for the Brethren to moralize upon, while the other three jewels are transferable from one Brother to another at the periodical changes of officers.

In the Hebrew "Book of Creation," the "Sepher Yetzirah," the Hexad is spoken of: the units representing the four quarters of the World; North, South, East, and West, and also height and depth, and in the midst of all is the Holy Temple. See my translation; cap. i. v. 11, and notes. Third Edition. 1911.

The Druids had a mysterious religious preference for the number 6. They performed their principal ceremonies on the 6th day of the moon, and on the 6th day of the moon began their year. They went 6 together to gather the sacred mistletoe (misseltoe), and in monuments and plates now extant we often find 6 of their priests grouped together. See Mayo, ii. 239.

An astronomical period of 600 years, spoken of as the "Naros," the Cycle of the Sun, the Luni-Solar period or Sibylline year, consisting of 31 periods of 19 years, and one of 11 years, is often referred to in old works on the Mysteries. It seems to have been known by the Chaldeans and ancient Indians; it is a period of peculiar properties. Cassini, a great astronomer, declares it the most perfect of all astronomic periods.

If on a certain day at noon, a new moon took place at any certain point in the heavens, it would take place again at the expiration of 600 years, at the same place and time, and with the planets all in similar positions.

It is supposed that one recurrence of this period is referred to in the 4th Eclogue of Virgil, the poem, which, as is well known, has been spoken of as containing an allusion to the Messiah, Jesus.

"The period sung by the Cumæan Sibyl has now arrived, and the grand series of ages (that series which occurs again and again in the course of a mundane revolution) begins afresh. The virgin Astræa returns, another reign of Saturn commences, and a new progeny descends from heaven."

It has been calculated by the late Dr. Kenealy that a Messiah, or divine teacher, has been sent to the world every 600 years, thus:—

Adam, the first messenger from the Gods to our race on earth.

Enoch, the second, 600 years after.

Fo-hi, the third, to China in particular.

Brighou, a Hindoo prophet.

Zaratusht, Zoroaster, the fifth, to Persia.

Thoth, Taautus, or Hermes Trismegistus, sent to the Egyptians.

Amosis, or Moses the Jewish law-giver, the seventh.

Lao Tseu, a second to China, 600 B.C., the eighth.

Jesus the ninth, to the Jews first and then to the Gentiles.

Mohammed the tenth; he flourished about A.D. 600.

Chengiz Khan the eleventh, A.D. 1 zoo, conquered Persia.

Who the special messenger of 1800 was, the author is ignorant.

The secrets of the Naros of the Apocalypse and of the Mediatorial Sacrifice have been considered the secrets of the Ancient Mysteries. Circumcision was possibly an outward sign of Initiation in the earliest times.

Jesus, at any rate, writes the Author of the "Book of God," appeared at the 9th Naros, and no one can deny that such a messenger was expected. Juvenal, oddly enough too, mentions in

Satire XI II. v. 28, "Nona ætas igitur"—"now is the ninth age"—which indeed it was, though how he knew it, is a mystery.

The Sothic Cycle was 1461 years, containing 18,000 lunations.

N.B.—Naros is not to be confused with "Saros," a cycle of the moon of 18 years and 10 days, which was known to the Chaldeans and Greeks, a period after the expiry of which the eclipses of the moon recur similarly: it consists of 223 lunations.

The circumference of a globe has been fixed at 360 degrees, six sixties; the hour divided into 60 minutes, each of 60 seconds. The Tartars had a period of 60 days, the Chinese also; and the Asiatics generally a period of 60 years. The Babylonian great period was 3600 years, the Naros multiplied by 6.

The "Lily" which in all the old Annunciation pictures Gabriel presents to the Virgin has 6 leaves, and the flower shows 6 petals all alike, around a central three-headed stigma, as is botanically correct. One of the three main divisions into which plants are arranged by Botanists, is typified by a predominance of the numbers 3 and 6, in all parts of the flowers, 6 leaves forming a perianth, 6 stamens, and a 3-lobed stigma with a 3- or 6-celled ovary is the common arrangement.

Berosus, one of the Chaldean Priests, mentions three periods of time, a Sossus of 60 years; a Naros, or Neros, of 600 years, and the Saros, 3600 years. There seems some confusion here with the Saros of 18 years and 10 days.

Bailly, in his "Astronomie Ancienne," p. 31, says: The Brahmins used the numbers 60 and 3600 in computing time. The Chaldeans also did so. The Brahmins have also an Antediluvian period of 600 years. The Tartars and Chinese also used a period of 60 years in their computations of time.

Under the number, Six, too, we must not omit to mention the symbol of the double triangle, Hexapla, or Hexalpha, the Shield of David, it is used at present as a sign in the Degree of the Royal Arch in England. It must not be confused with the Pentalpha which is the true Solomon's seal. In Christian Churches we find the Hexalpha used to express the union of the Divine and human natures, deemed to exist in Jesus, the Christ of the New Testament. The blending of the two triangles has also been used to typify the union of Fire and Water; for the early symbol of Fire was the triangle apex upward, and that of Water the same apex downward: the symbols of Air and Earth were two similar triangles, each with a cross bar.

The Talmud says:—

Six things are disgraceful to a wise man; to walk alone at night; to scent oneself for walking by day; to talk with a strange woman in the street; to talk at table with the ignorant; to wear ragged shoes, and to be late at the house of prayer. Berachoth, 43. 2.

Six things lay up capital for hereafter, and also bear interest in this world; hospitality well ordered; comfort to the sick; prayerful meditation; early instruction of children; training in the Mosaic law, and charitable treatment of a neighbour. Sabbat. 127. 1.

Evil Demons have 6 characters; like men they take food and drink, they beget and they die; like angels, they have wings, they pass from one end of the world to the other, and they can learn the future. Talmud.

Solomon is called by six names; Solomon, Jedidiah, Koheleth, son of Jakeh, Agur and Lemuel: see "The Fathers," "Aboth," by Rabbi Nathan.

There are 6 kinds of Fire,—common fire which eats and does not drink; fire that drinks and does not eat, as fever; fire that eats and drinks, that of Elijah, 1 Kings xviii. 38; the fire on the Altar which consumed both moist and dry; the fire of Gabriel which consumed other fire, and the Essential fire of God which consumed evil angels. Yoma, 21. 2.

The Tables of Moses were said to have been 6 hands-breadths long, 6 wide and 3 thick. Talmud; Nedarim, 38. 8. Hershon reckons that if cut out of Sinaitic stone, each Table would have weighed 28 tons, but he is in error, reckoning hands-breadths as ells, as 18 inches instead of 4 inches.

The Angel of Death had no power over 6 holy persons; Abraham, Isaac, Jacob, Moses, Aaron and Miriam. Bava Bathra, 17. 1. These died by the Divine Kiss of death, but it is not so definitely stated in the case of Miriam, for fear of scandal.

The Lion has 6 names in the Book of Job; ARI, ShchL, KPIR, LISh, LBIA and ShChTz.

The Serpent has 6 names; NChSh, OKShUB, APOH, TzPOUNI, TNIN and ShRP. Nachash the Brazen Serpent; Okeshub, an asp, Psalm cxxiv. 4; Opoh, an adder, Isaiah xli. 24; Tzephouni, the basilisk, Isaiah xiv. 29; Tanin, the serpent or crocodile; and Seraph, a serpent of fire. See Rabbi Nathan, cap. 29.

Six blasts of the Horn were blown on the eve of the Sabbath, and then the Sabbath had begun.

W. F. Shaw says that 6 is the number of temptation and sin, for at the 6th hour of the 6th day the first temptation came into the world. Six is the number of toil and work, for 6 days the Israelites had to collect manna; at the 6th hour of-the 6th day Jesus was sentenced to death, and in the Revelations the 6th seal, trumpet and vial were all emblematic of woe. The Flood came when Noah was 600 years old.

The number 666 was an emblem of the Great Wicked One, still without identification, but he is implied in a prototype, Schechem ben Hamor, whose name is 666 by Gematria, ShKM BN ChMVR, he was the corruptor of Dinah. See Genesis xxxiv. verse 2.

The Jews expected that the end of the present dispensation of the world would arrive after 6000 years, and St. Barnabas repeats this as a reasonable belief of the ancient Christian Church.

The Ancient Egyptians had for their highest Priests a College of 6, of which hardly any information has come down to us; but one Aseshra is mentioned as Master of the Mysterious Words of the 6, and a statue has been found of one Ei-meri, whose engraved title is Chief of the Dwelling of the Great Six.

THE HEPTAD. 7.

THE Heptad, say the followers of "Pythagoras," was so called from the Greek verb "sebo," to venerate (and from the Hebrew ShBO, seven, or satisfied, abundance), being Septos, "Holy," "divine," and "motherless," and a "Virgin."

From Nicomachus we learn that it was called "Minerva," being unmarried and virginal, begotten neither by a mother, *i.e.*, even number, nor from a father, *i.e.*, odd number: but proceeding from the summit of the Father of all things, the Monad; even as Minerva sprang all armed from the Forehead of Jove or Zeus.

Hence also Obrimopatrë, or daughter of a mighty father, and Glaucopis, shining-eyed, and αμητωρ and αγελεια, Ametor and Ageleia, she that carries off the spoil.

And "Fortune," for it decides mortal affairs.

And "Voice," for there are seven tones in every voice, human and instrumental: because they are emitted by the seven planets, and form the Music of the Spheres.

Also Tritogenia, because there are 3 parts of the Soul, the Intellectual, Irascible and Epithymetic (desiring), and 4 most perfect virtues are produced. Just as of the three intervals, length, breadth, and depth, there are four boundaries in corporeal existence—point, line, superficies and solid.

It is called "Agelia," from Agelai, herds, as groups of stars were called by the Babylonian sages, over which herds ruled 7 angels.

Also Phylakikos, φυλακικος = preserving, "guardian," because the Seven Planets direct and guide our universe.

Also Ægis, from Pallas Athene, or Minerva, the bearer of the breast-plate or ægis, also Telesphoros, leading to the end, because the 7th month is prolific; and Judgment, because their Physicians looked for a crisis on the 7th day in many diseases.

Among other curious problems and speculations, the Pythagorean philosophers attempted to prove that offspring born at the full term, 9 months, or at 7 months, were viable, *i.e.*, might be reared, but not those born at 8 months, because 8 consists of two odd numbers (male only) 5 and 3; but in 9 and 7, male and female numbers are united, as 5 + 4 = 9 and 4 + 3 = 7, whilst eight can only be divided into two odd or two evens, *i.e.*, similar sexed numbers.

In respect to life and its divisions, they remarked the ages are measured by the number 7.

In the first 7 years the teeth are erupted.

second 7 years comes on ability to emit prolific seed.

third 7 years, the growth of the beard as manhood.

fourth 7 years, strength reaches its maximum.

fifth 7 years is the season for marriage.

sixth 7 years, the height of intelligence arrives.

seventh 7 years, the maturity of reason.

eighth 7 years, perfection of both.

ninth 7 years, equity and mildness, passions become gentle.

tenth 7 years, the end of desirable life.

Solon the Athenian Lawgiver, and Hippocrates the physician, also used this 7-year division of life.

Solon

The Pleiades, a group of seven stars in the constellation Taurus, was thought of mighty power over earthly destiny; there were seven also of the Hyades, daughters of Atlas; and the seven stars which guided the sailors. Ursa Major, in which the Hindoos locate the Sapta Rishi, seven sages of primitive wisdom, are a group of the first importance and are easily recognised.

Duncan, in his "Astro-Theology," gives 7 stages of life with associated planets; thus, Infancy, Moon, Luna; Childhood, Mercury, Knowledge; Youth, Venus, Love; Manhood, Sol; Full Strength, Mars; Maturity of Judgment, Jupiter; and Old Age, Saturn.

Some philosophers have said that our souls have 7 foci in the material body, viz., the five senses, the voice, and the generative power.

The body has seven obvious parts, the head, chest, abdomen, two legs and two arms.

There are seven internal organs, stomach, liver, heart, lungs, spleen and two kidneys.

The ruling part, the head, has seven parts for external use, two eyes, two ears, two nostrils and a mouth.

There are seven things seen, body, interval, magnitude, colour, motion and permanency.

There are seven inflections of the voice, the acute, grave, circumflex, rough, smooth, the long and the short sounds.

The hand makes seven motions; up and down, to the right and left, before and behind, and circular.

There are seven evacuations;—tears from the eyes, mucus of the nostrils, the saliva, the semen, two excretions and the perspiration.

Modern medical knowledge corroborates the ancient dictum that in the seventh month the human offspring becomes viable.

Menstruation tends to occur in series of four times seven days, and is certainly related to Luna in an occult manner.

The lyre has 7 strings, corresponding to the planets.

There are 7 vowels in English and some other tongues.

Theon of Smyrna also notices that an average length of an adult's intestine is 28 feet, four times seven, and 28 also is a perfect number.

The number 7 is also associated with Voice and Sound, with Clio the Muse; with Osiris the Egyptian deity; with Nemesis, Fate,—Adrastia, not to be escaped from; and with Mars.

As to the sacredness of the number 7, note among the Hebrews, oaths were confirmed by seven witnesses; or by seven victims offered in sacrifice; as see the covenant between Abraham and Abimelech with seven lambs, Genesis, chap. xxi. vv. 28, 21–28; the Hebrew word seven, also Sh B O H, is derived from, or is a similar to Sh B O, to swear.

Clean beasts were admitted into the ark by sevens, whilst the unclean only in pairs.

The Goths had 7 Deities from whom come our names of week days; Sun, Moon, Tuisco, Wotan, Thor, Friga, Seatur, corresponding, of course, to the planets.

Apollo, the Sun God, had a Greek title Ebdomaios, sevenfold.

The Persian Mithras, a Sun God, had the number 7 sacred to him.

Mithras

Note the Mysterious Kadosh Ladder of 7 steps ascent and 7 steps descent, the one side Oheb Eloah, Love of God; the other Oheb Kerobo, love of the neighbour.

Plato, in his "Timæus," teaches that from the number seven was generated the Soul of the World, *Anima Mundana* (Adam Kadmon).

The seven wise men of Greece were:

Bias who said, "Most men are bad," B.C. 550.

Chilo ,, "Consider the end," B.C. 590.

Cleobūlos ,, "Avoid Extremes," B.C. 580.

Periander ,, "Nothing is impossible to perseverance," B.C. 600.

Pittâcus ,, "Know thy opportunity," B.C. 569.

Solon ,, "Know thyself," B.C. 600.

Thāles ,, "Suretyship is ruin," B.C. 550.

The Seven Wonders of the World are thus enumerated:

1. Pyramids of Egypt.

2. The hanging Gardens of Babylon, for Semiramis.

3. Tomb of Mausōlus, King of Caria, at Halicarnassus, built by Artemisia, his Queen.

4. Temple of Diana at Ephesus, 552 B.C. Ctesiphon was the chief architect.

5. Colossus of Rhodes, an image of the sun god, Apollo, of brass, 290 B.C.

6. Statue of Zeus, at Athens, by Phidias.

7. Pharos of Egypt, built by Ptolemy Philadelphus, of white marble, 283 B.C.; or the Palace of Cyrus which is sometimes substituted.

Sanskrit lore has very frequent reference to this number: note:—

Sapta Rishi, seven sages; Sapta Kula, 7 castes; Sapta Loka, seven worlds; Sapta Para, 7 cities; Sapta Dwipa, seven holy islands; Sapta Arania, 7 deserts; Sapta Parna, 7 human principles; Sapta Samudra, seven holy seas; Sapta Vruksha, 7 holy trees.

The Assyrian Tablets also teem with groups of sevens—7 gods of sky; 7 gods of earth; 7 gods of fiery spheres: seven gods maleficent; seven phantoms; spirits of seven heavens; spirits of seven earths.

The Chaldean notion seems to have been that 7 was a holy number which became nefast under certain conditions. The opposite sides of a die added together are always seven in total numeration, the 4 opposite 3, 6 opposite 1, and so on.

It used to be asserted, says John Heydon, that every seventh Male born without any female coming between, can cure the King's Evil, by Word, or Touch.

St. James iii. 17 gives the 7 characters of wisdom.

After Birth the 7th hour decides whether the child will live, in 7 days the cord falls off, in twice 7 days the eyes follow a light, thrice 7 days turns the head, 7 months gets teeth, twice 7 months sits firmly, thrice 7 months begins to talk, after 4 times 7 months walks strongly.

After 7 years, teeth of second set appear.

After 14 years is the arrival of generative power. After 2i the hair of Manhood is completed.

After 28 we cease to grow, at 35 is greatest strength, at 49 is the greatest discretion, and 70 is the natural end of Life.

The Moon passes through stages of 7 days in increase, full, decrease, and renewal.

Naaman was ordered by Elisha (an Adept) to take seven dips in Jordan, to cleanse himself from Leprosy.

The Golden Candlestick of Seven Branches was a notable emblematic ornament of the Tabernacle of Moses, Exodus xxv. 31.

Note the seven years for Repentance; 7 churches of Asia (or Assiah), 7 Angels with Trumpets, 7 candlesticks of the Holy Places, 7 seals, 7 trumpets, 7 kings, 7 thousands slain, 7 vials of wrath to be poured out, pace the Apocalypse. 7 members make a Freemasons' lodge perfect, although 5 may hold one.

Francis Barrett, in his "Magus," catalogues 7 Birds, Fishes, Animals, metals, stones, and members of the body.

It has been said there are seven apertures of the skull to correspond with the planets.

There are Seven Degrees in the Oriental Order of Sikha and the Sat Bhai (7 Brothers); but I have doubts of the Brahmanic authenticity of the present Order of the name, which was introduced by J. H. Lawrence Archer.

From the relative length of their courses the ancients constructed a Planetary Ladder, with Vowel Symbols, thus:

Moon	Merc.	Venus	Sun	Mars	Jupit.	Saturn
a	e	ee	i	o	u	oo

These symbols were used in mystical knowledge, As an Inscription at the Temple of Apollo at Delphi shows, where E I meant the Sun and its nearest Planet, *i.e.*, Sun and Mercury; and Mercury was often represented as a Dog, following a Sun Man.

The Oracle of Claros (Macrobius, Saturnalia, 1. 18) said that IAΩ (the Gnostic Deity) was the Sun and the first and last of the planetary set, hence the 7 Concentric spheres.

Duncan assigns these Minerals and Animals to the 7 Heavenly Bodies known to the ancient world.

Moon, Bull, Silver

Mercury, Serpent, Quicksilver

Venus, Dove, Copper

Sun, Lion, Gold

Mars, Wolf, Iron

Jupiter, Eagle, Pewter

Saturn, Ass, Lead

Note also the number of 7 pipes in the Musical instrument at the mouth of the old deity Pan, the Great Whole, a Sun God (not the later Rural Pan).

An ancient symbol of the universe was a Ship with seven pilots, in the centre of the ship, a Lion; possibly from an idea that the Sun first rose in Leo.

Note Aries supplanted Taurus, as the constellation in which the sun rises at the Vernal equinox; Taurus was the sign at the early fabulous periods of the earth—it was displaced about 300 B.C. The sign becomes changed every 2150 years by the precession of the equinoxes: Pisces has now followed Aries; but the Sun is still said to enter the sign Aries at the Vernal Equinox about March 21st. Its actual position in March 1900 was near *omega* Pisces.

T. Subba Row describes the Seven Primary Forces of Nature as six powers resumed in a seventh. These are called Sakti (Mahamaya) and are related to Kanya, *i.e.*, Virgo, as the 6th Zodiacal Sign; they are Parasakti, force of light and heat; Inanasakti, intellect; Itchasakti, cause of voluntary movements; Kriyasakti, energy of will; Kundalini sakti, the life force shown in attraction and repulsion, positive and negative; Mantrika sakti, the power of sounds, vibration, music, words and speech; these are summarized in Daivi prakriti = the Light of the Logos.

Our physical senses known as 5, are an incomplete set, there are indeed 7 forms or modes of perception, as appears in the highest developments of the "Chabrat zereh aur bokher," and as described in the oldest Sanskrit occult science of the Upanishads:—smell, taste, sight, touch, hearing—and 6th, Mental perception, with 7th, spiritual understanding: the two latter were not dwarfed and materialized into noticeable organs in this fifth Race of beings, to which Man now belongs. For a fuller explanation see the "Secret Doctrine" of H. P. Blavatsky. The Archaic scheme recognized Seven States of Matter;—homogeneous, aeriform, nebulous or curdlike, atomic, germinal fiery elemental, fourfold vapoury, and lastly that which is cold and dependent on a vivifying Sun for light and heat.

Our Earth, symbolised by MALKUTH of the Kabalah, is the seventh of a series, and is on the Fourth plane; it is generated by Jesod, the foundation the Sixth World, and after complete purification will in the 7th Race of the 7th Cycle become re-united to the Spiritual Logos and in the end to the Absolute. Our earth has been already thrice changed, and each cycle sees seven kings (as of Edom). There were Seven Kings of Edom, Genesis, xxxvi. v. 31; the Kabalists consider these as types of primordial worlds which failed to survive their creation. Seven is the key to the Mosaic creation, as to the symbols of every religion. There are Seven Planes of being, the upper three are subjective and unknowable to mankind, the lower four are objective and may be contemplated by man as metaphysical abstractions: so there are the seven Principles in Man, and the upper triad are parted from the lower group of four at dissolution.

The Seven Principles constituting man are variously named by the Esoteric Buddhism, by the Vedantic scheme, and by other philosophies, but they correspond in idea; first from above come Atma, a ray from the Absolute; Buddhi, spiritual soul; and Manas, human soul; these are the superior triad, which separates at human death from the lower tetrad of principles. The lower four are Kama rupa, the passions; Linga Sarira, tile astral body; Prana, life essence; and Sthula Sarira, the lower body; see the dogmas of Esoteric Buddhism.

The Kabalah divides these into four planes of the Soul, which are further separated by adepts; these are Chiah, Neshamah, Ruach and Nephesh, which correspond to the symbolical worlds of Atziluth, Briah, Yetzirah and Assiah.

There is an occult reference in the Seven stars in the head of Taurus called the Pleiades, six present and one hidden—said to be daughters of Atlas, who, pursued by Orion, were changed by Zeus in mercy into pigeons (peleia). The missing one is Merope, who married the mortal Sisyphus, and hides herself for shame.

Seven was the number of the Rabbis who left the "Greater Holy Assembly"; ten had formed it, three had passed away from the "Sod," SVD, mystery. See "The Greater" and "Lesser Holy Assembly," or the Ha Idra Rabba Quadisha and Ha Idra Suta Quadisha.

Athanasius Kircher the Jesuit states that the ancient Egyptians associated numbers to the planets as follows:—

Saturn	3, 9, 15, 45
Jupiter	4, 16, 34, 136
Mars	5, 25, 65, 325
Sol	6, 36, 111, 666
Venus	7, 49, 145, 1225
Mercury	8, 64, 260, 2080
Luna	9, 81, 369, 3521

In this matter see also Francis Barrett, "The Magus."

The later Coptic names of the 7 Gods and planets and Genii of the World of the Ancient Egyptians are: Saturn, Rephan, God of time; Jupiter, Picheus, God of life; Mars, Moloch, God of destruction; Sol, Phre or Pire, meaning Holy Lord; Venus, Suroth, lady of love; Mercury, Hermes, Hermanubis, God of speech; and Luna, Piooh, lady of the waters.

In China 7 is the number of Death, and their days of mourning are 7 times 7: the Seven Star Plank is the name of the bottom plank of a coffin in which they bore 7 holes.

The Hindoos speak of 7 Tatwas, the abstract principles of existence, metaphysical and physical, the subtle elements and the corresponding human senses, of which only five are yet developed. So there are five exoteric, Akasa, Vayu, Tejas, Apas and Prithwi; the first two esoteric yet unknown are Ani and Anupadaka. The first name means One, Unity, the Atom, and is a name of Brahma; the latter means parentless, self-existent. The first five are referred to primeval Aether, Air, Fire, Water and Earth: and to Hearing, Touch, Sight, Taste and Smell; note Air is not Hearing. See Rama Prasad on "The Tatwas."

The Sanscrit names of the Seven Planets used in Hindoo Astrology are Surya for the Sun, Chandra for Moon, Kuja for Mars, Budhan for Mercury, Guru for Jupiter, Sukra for Venus, and Shani for Saturn: then there are Rahu, the upper Lunar Node, and Ketu for the lower. Jupiter is also named Brihaspati.

The word Septemtriones refers to the north, and is so called from its reference to the 7 stars of Ursa Major, also called the Plough, and seen in the Zodiac of Denderah as the Thigh.

The Talmudic Berachoth, 14. 1, says he who passes 7 nights without dreaming deserves to be called wicked.

The Kabalists describe Seven classes of Angels: Ishim, Arelim, Chashmalim, Melakim, Auphanim, Seraphim and Kerubim.

The Judaic Hell was given seven names by the Kabalists; Sheol, Abaddon, Tihahion, Bar Shacheth, Tzelmuth, Shaari Muth, and Gehinnom.

Seven things were formed before the world; Law, Repentance, Paradise, Gehenna (that is Gai hinnom), the Throne of Glory, and the Messiah. The Targum Yerushalmi says these were formed 2000 years before the World's creation. Talmud, Pesachim, 54. 1.

Seven things were hidden from man; the day of death, the time of the resurrection, the final judgment, the opinion of his fellow-man, the time of the Jewish restoration, and the Fall of Persia (whatever that may mean). Pesachim, 54. 2.

The Talmud in "Chagijah" names 7 Heavens, and Occultists recognize 7 Planetary Heavens; Raquie, Zebul, Makum, Maon, Sagun, Ghereboth, and Shamaim.

In Micah, chapter v. verse 5, we read that 7 shepherds shall waste Assyria; the Talmud says they were Adam, Jacob and Methuselah, Abraham, Jacob and Moses, and David. Succah. 52. 2

Of Prophetesses there were 7;—Sarah, Miriam, Deborah, Hannah, Abigail, Huldah and Esther.

In the Talmud, Kethuboth, 17. 1, it is said that it is permissible to the Jew to look into his wife's face for 7 days after marriage; after this it is presumably wrong, in their opinion.

On the 7th day of the month Adar, Moses died and the rain of manna ceased, says the Talmud, but this appears to be contradicted in Joshua v. verses 10–12. He was born on the same day of the same month.

The Bava Kama says that after 7 years a male hyæna becomes a bat, in another 7 years a Vampire, after another a Thorn, and after another is turned into a demon. If a man fails to pray devoutly for 7 years, his spine after death becomes a serpent.

Besides those who prophesied for Israel, there were 7 other prophets, Beor, Balaam, Job, Eliphaz, Bildad, Zohar, and Elihu the son of Barachel the Buzite.

The Bava Bathra says that 7 men form an unbroken series to this day. Adam was seen by Methuselah, then Shem, Jacob, Amram, Ahijah the Shilonite, and Elijah, who saw him, and Elijah is still alive until to-day.

Even 7 years of pestilence will not cause a man to die before his allotted time. This dictum of the treatise Sanhedrin is a statement of predestination.

A Ram has but one voice while alive, but after death his body makes 7 sounds; his horns make two trumpets, his thigh bones two pipes, his skin will cover a drum, the large intestines are formed into strings for the lyre, and the small intestines will make the small strings for the harp.

In the Sabbat, 152. 2, of the Talmud it is said that the Soul of a man watches over his corpse for 7 days. Compare this with the Theosophic teaching that the Linga Sarira broods over the body for a week after death.

Rabbi Nathan says that 7 good qualities avail at the Judgment; wisdom, righteousness, good opinions, mercy, truth, grace, and peace. Seven epithets are applied to the Earth in the Hebrew tongue; Aretz, Adamah, Arequa, Gia, Tziah, Yabeshah, Cheled or Thebel. The mystical River Sambatyon flowed all the week, but was still on the 7th day, says Rashi. Hershon, Talmudic Miscellany, 154.

The 7 Catholic Deadly Sins are Pride, covetousness, lust, anger, gluttony, envy and sloth.

The Seven Deadly Sins

The 7 Gifts of the Holy Spirit, Isaiah xi. v. 2, are Wisdom, Understanding, Counsel, Fortitude, Knowledge, Piety and Fear of the Lord; these are seven of the Kabalistic Sephiroth.

Seven is the token of Union between God, who is Triune, and Man, who is Quaternary. W. F. Shaw.

The Holy Ghost is said to impart a 7-fold gift; 7 Lamps burn before the Throne of God.

The Council of Arles declared that 1 Bishops ought to take part in the Ordination of a Bishop.

There was a 7 years' probation for admission to the Celtic Order of the Culdees. There are 7 Vestments of the Christian priesthood, and Bishops should wear 7 others, Sandals, Dalmatic, Rational, Mitre, Gloves, Ring and Staff.

The 7 Champions of Christendom were St. George for England, St. Denis of France, St. James of Spain, St. Andrew of Scotland, St. David of Wales, St. Patrick of Ireland, and St. Antonio of Italy.

The 7 Sleepers of Ephesus, according to the monkish legend, were Christians who hid in a cave under the persecutions of Decius in the Third Century; they fell into a trance and slept 200 years. They awaked in A.D. 447 and going to the Emperor Theodosius II., they convinced him of the truth of the Life beyond the grave: this done, they returned to the cave to sleep until the Last Judgment.

The 7 Dolours of the Virgin Mary is the name of a Roman Catholic Fast Day held on the Friday before Palm Sunday.

The 7 Wise Masters were officers of King Kurush who tell stories to save the life of the King's son: they exist in Greek, Syriac, Hebrew, Persian, and in English are called The Book of Sindibad, edited by Clouston.

The Coptic Gnostics represented the Jehovah of the Hebrews by a curious arrangement of the 7 vowels, without a consonant; thus IEHOOUA (the H is the Greek eta, long e; and the first O is the Greek long O, omega).

In the Zoroastrian theology we read of the highest beings the 7 Amshaspands; Ormuzd, source of life; Bahman, the king of this world; Ardibehest, fire producer; Shahrivar, the former of metals; Spandarmat, queen of the earth (the Gnostic Sophia); Khordad, the ruler of times and seasons; and Amerdad, ruling over the vegetable world. Below there are the 27 Izeds, ruled over by Mithras; in opposition to these were powers of darkness, the 7 arch devs, and the 27 devs, or devils as we call them.

The historic city of Rome, pagan before it was Christian, was built upon Seven Hills; the Palatine, Cœlian, Aventine, Viminal, Quirinal, Esquiline, and the Capitol. In Latin times it was called Urbs Septicollis. Some old authors speak of "Valentia" as a secret name for Rome.

The "Bijou Notes and Queries," vol. xiv., p. 235, says that the 7 days of the week have all been used as sacred days; Sunday by Christians; Monday by the Greeks; Tuesday by the Persians; Wednesday by the Assyrians; Thursday by the Egyptians; Friday by the Turks; and Saturday by the Jews.

The number 7 was curiously related to H. P. Blavatsky and the Theosophical Society. "Lucifer" was first published in 1887, and 1887 is the sum of 17 hundreds, 17 tens, and 17 units; H. P. B. lived at 17 Lansdowne Road, and 17 Avenue Road; "Lucifer" was published at 7 Duke Street; 7 volumes were completed at her death; Colonel Olcott first met her at 7 Beckman Street, and later at 71 Broadway, New York. Anna Kingsford was elected president first of the London T. S. Lodge on 7th January 1883; "Isis Unveiled" was published in 1877, and the Third volume of the "Secret Doctrine" was published in 1897, after her death.

THE OGDOAD. 8.

Is the first cube of energy, and is the only evenly even number within the decad. The Greeks thought it an all-powerful number; they had a Proverb "all things are eight."

Camerarius, in his edition of the Arithmetic of Nicomachus, calls it Universal Harmony, because musical ratios are distinguished by this number.

The Ratio of 9 to 8 is sesquioctave, this forms a tone and is attributed to the Moon.

Mercury.

12 to 9 is sesquitertian

12 to 8 is sesquialter

Venus.

16 to 12 is sesquitertian

16 to 8 is duple

Sun.

18 to 12 is sesquialter.

18 to 9 is duple

Mars.

21 to 9 is duple sesquitertian

Attributed to Jupiter.

24 to 18 is sesquitertian

24 to 12 is duple.

24 to 8 is triple

18 to 12 sesquialter

12 to 8 sesquialter

Saturn.

32 to 24 sesquitertian

32 to 8 quadruple

Are ascribed to the 8th or Inerratic Sphere which comprehends all the rest.

36 to 24. sesquialter

36 to 18 duple

36 to 8 quadruple

24 to 18 sesquitertian

Hence the Ogdoad was also called "Cadmeia," because Harmony was looked upon as the wife of Cadmus; and Cadmus meant the Sub-lunary World, as Olympiodorus says. Eight was called also Mother, and Rhea, Cybele and Dindymene, from being the first cube, and a cube representing the earth.

The eight persons saved from the flood of Xisuthrus are synonyms of many octaves of gods, such as the 8 Cabiri great gods of Samothrace; see Bryant and Faber on this myth.

There are 8 Beatitudes of the Christian religion, Matthew, chap. v.

Eight is the number of the Moons of Saturn.

There have been several Masonic orders concerned with this Noachite Ogdoad, as the Prussian masons, Knights of the Royal Axe, or Prince of Libanus, the Noachites, and the Royal Ark Mariners, which is a subsidiary order to the Mark Master Masons.

Macrobius says the Ogdoad was the type of Justice, because it consists of evenly even numbers, and on account of its equal divisions.

John Heydon tells us that 8 Events befall the Damned, and that there are 8 rewards of the Blessed.

The number 8 was sacred to Dionysos, who was born at the 8th month; the isle of Naxos was dedicated to him and it was granted to the women of Naxos, that their children born in the 8th month should live, whereas it is usual for such to die, although those born in either the 7th or the 9th month are usually reared.

The Jews were accustomed to practise Circumcision on male infants upon the 8th day after birth.

The Jews at the Chanucah or Feast of Dedication lit 8 candles, and it lasted 8 days. This is the Engkainia of John x. 22. As to conjuring among the ancient Jews, it is said in Talmud, Succah. 53. 1, that Levi played with 8 knives; Samuel in the presence of the King Sapor of Persia used 8 cups, and Abaji before Rabbi Rava used 8 eggs.

Eight prophets were descended from Rahab the Harlot, viz., Neraiah, Seraiah, Maasiah, Jeremiah, Hilkiah, Hannemeel, and Shallum. Note also that Huldah the prophetess was the grandchild of Rahab.

The last 8 verses of Deuteronomy, The Mosaic Law, The Pentateuch, were written by Joshua. Bava Bathra, 14. 1.

Rabbi Nathan states that there were 8 sects of the Pharisees: but both of the Talmuds (Jerusalem and Babylon) name only seven. It is prophesied that the Harps which will be played on earth before the Messiah will have 8 strings. Erachin, 13. 2.

As seven was the number of the original Creation, so 8, says W. F. Shaw, may be considered as the Day of Regeneration. Eight souls were saved in the Ark of Noah, and Noah was the 8th in descent, his name was NVCh = 8 times 8 = 64.

888 is the special number of Jesus Christ as "He who is the Resurrection and the Life." He is the great opponent of the 666, the number of the Beast, the number of a Man.

The ancient Chinese writings refer to 8 musical sounds, the Pah-yin. (G. Schlegel.)

THE ENNEAD. 9.

THE Ennead is the first square of an odd number, it was said to be like the Ocean flowing around the other numbers within the Decad; no further elementary number is possible, hence it is like the Horizon because all the numbers are bounded by it. We find that it was called Prometheus, and "Freedom from Strife," and "Vulcan," because the ascent of numbers is as far as 9, just as the ascent of things decomposed by fire is as far as the sphere of Fire (the summit of the air), and Juno, because the Sphere of the air is arranged according to the novenary system, and "sister and wife to Jupiter" from its conjunction with the Monad. And "Telesphoros" or "Bringing to an end" because the human offspring is carried 9 calendar months by the parent. And *teleios* or perfect for the same reason, and also called "Perfect" because it is generated from the Triad, which is called "Perfect."

Attention is called to its being an emblem of Matter, which, ever varying, is never destroyed; so the number 9 when multiplied by any number always reproduces itself, thus:—9 times 2 are 18 and 8 plus 1 are nine: and so on as below:

$9 \times 3 = 27; 2 + 7 = 9$ $9 \times 12 = 108; 1 + 8 + 0 = 9$

$9 \times 4 = 36; 3 + 6 = 9$ $9 \times 13 = 117; 7 + 1 + 1 = 9$

$9 \times 5 = 45; 4 + 5 = 9$ $9 \times 14 = 126; 6 + 2 + 1 = 9$

$9 \times 6 = 54; 5 + 4 = 9$ $9 \times 15 = 135; 5 + 3 + 1 = 9$

$9 \times 7 = 63; 6 + 3 = 9$ $9 \times 16 = 144; 4 + 4 + 1 = 9$

$9 \times 8 = 72; 7 + 2 = 9$ $9 \times 17 = 153; 3 + 5 + 1 = 9$

$9 \times 9 = 81; 8 + 1 = 9$ $9 \times 18 = 162; 2 + 6 + 1 = 9$

$9 \times 10 = 90; 9 + 0 = 9$ $9 \times 19 = 171; 1 + 7 + 1 = 9$

$9 \times 11 = 99;$ $9 \times 20 = 180; 8 + 1 + 0 = 9$

In John Heydon's "Holy Guide," 1662, we find that he asserts the number 9 to have other curious properties:—"If writ or engraved on Silver, or Sardis, and carried with one, the wearer becomes invisible, as Caleron, the Brother-in-law of Alexander, did, and by this means lay with his Brother's concubines as often as he did himself. Nine also obtaineth the love of Women. At the 9th hour our Saviour breathed his last; on the ninth day the ancients buried their dead; after 9 years Numa received his laws from Jove; note the 9 cubits length of the *iron* bedstead of the giant Og, king of Basan, who is a type of the Devil, and there are 9 orders of Devils in Sheol (what we call Hell). It prevails against Plagues and Fevers; it causes Long life and Health, and by it Plato so ordered events that he died at the age of nine times 9."

There are nine orders of Angels, says Gregory, A.D. 381, in Homily 34: Seraphim, Cherubim, Thrones, Dominions, Virtues, Powers, Principalities, Archangels and Angels.

From a Christian point of view the numbers represent:—

1. Unity of the Godhead.

2. The hypostatic union of Christ.

3. Trinity.

4. Evangelists.

5. Wounds of Jesus.

6. Is the number of sin.

7. Gifts of the spirit, Rev. i. 12; and Jesus 7 times spoke on the cross.

8. Beatitudes.

9. Orders of Angels.

10. Commandments.

11. Apostles besides Judas.

12. Original Apostolic College

13. College completed by St. Paul.

The Nine Muses of ancient Greece were called daughters of Zeus and Mnemosyne (Memory), and were Calliope, poetry; Clio, history; Melpomene, tragedy; Euterpe, music; Erato, love, inspiration and pantomime; Terpsichore, dancing; Urania, astronomy; Thalia, comedy, and Polyhymnia, eloquence.

The Novensiles are the nine Sabine Gods: viz.—Hercules, Romulus, Æsculapius, Bacchus, Æneas, Vesta, Santa, Fortuna and Fides. The Sabines became merged with the Romans about 266 B.C.

The Nine gods of the Etruscans were Juno, Minerva, Tinia, Vulcan, Mars, Saturn, Hercules, Summanus and Vedius; the Etruscans also became united with the Romans.

Note in Macaulay's poem of "Horatius," "Lars Porsena of Clusium by the *nine* gods he swore," in 596 B.C. Lars Porsena led the Etruscans; they were then most powerful: from the Etruscans the Romans took much of their law, custom and superstition.

It is by nines that Eastern presents are given, when they would extend their magnificence to the greatest degree, as mentioned in Comte de Caylus, "Oriental Tales." 1743.

Barrett's "Magus" notes also 9 precious stones, 9 orders of devils, 9 choirs of angels—he copies from John Heydon.

Note in this connection the Nundinals of the Romans, who marked the days by letters into parcels of 8 days, and on every 9th day the people left their pursuits and went to the towns to market; hence the jocular Latin saying, *Tres mulieres Nundinas faciunt*. These nundinals are a type of our Dominical letters, a set of seven marking out the 8th days. The Romans also held a purification ceremony on male infants on the 9th day of life, hence the presiding goddess of this rite was called Nundina.

The Nones were one of the sets of days composing each calendar month. The Roman Novennalia was a feast in memory of the dead celebrated every 9th year. The Novendiale was an occasional Roman Catholic fast to avert calamities, from this arose the R.C. system of Neuvaines.

There is a Masonic order of "Nine Elected Knights," in which 9 roses, 9 lights and 9 knocks are used.

The Mahometans have 99 names of the deity. Some Jews have taught that God has 9 times descended to earth; 1st in Eden, 2nd at the confusion of tongues, 3rd at the destruction of Sodom, 4th to Moses at Horeb, 5th at Sinai, 6th to Balaam, 7th to Elisha, 8th in the Tabernacle, and 9th in the Temple at Jerusalem; and that his 10th coming as the Messiah will be final.

The ancients had a fear of the number Nine and its multiples, especially 81; they thought them of evil presage, indicating change and fragility.

At the 9th hour Jesus the Saviour died.

Nine is also "the earth under evil influences."

John Heydon in the "Holy Guide," and J. M. Ragon, in his "Maçonnerie Occulte," thus associate numbers with the Planets.

Sun 1 and 4, Moon 2 and 7, Jupiter 3, Mercury 5, Venus 6, Saturn 8, Mars 9.

and the Zodiacal Signs thus:—

1 Leo

2 Aquarius

3 Capricornus

4 Sagittarius

5 Cancer

6 Taurus

7 Aries

8 Libra

9 Scorpio

10 Virgo

11 Pisces

12 Gemini.

The First and the Second Temples of the Jews were both destroyed on the 9th day of the Jewish month Ab. On the 9th day of Ab modern Jews do not wear the Talith and Phylacteries until evening. The day should be spent in tears, and no good comes of work done on that day.

The Talmud in Soteh, 20. 1, says that a woman prefers one measure of fun to 9 of Pharisaic professional goodness.

Nine persons have entered *Alive* into the Jews' Paradise; Enoch, Elijah, Messiah, Eliezer the servant of Abraham, Hiram king of Tyre, Ebed Melek the Ethiop, Jabez the son of Jehuda the Prince, Bathia daughter of Pharaoh, and Sarah the daughter of Asher. Some Rabbis add Rabbi Yoshua son of Levi, but he entered not at the door, but climbed over the wall. See Kethuboth, 7. 2.

In the 145th Psalm we find 9 reasons for praising God.

The Great Eleusinian Mysteries were the successors of the Egyptian Mysteries of Isis and Osiris, and were celebrated at Eleusis and possibly also at Athens, in honour of Demeter or Ceres; they occupied 9 days, and were commenced on the fifteenth day of the third Attic month, Boedromion, September: they took place once in every five years.

The Lesser Mysteries were performed in the month Elaphebolion, March, at Agræ on the River Ilyssus in honour of Persephone or Proserpine, daughter of Ceres.

Candidates after reception became Mystæ: in the Greater Mysteries they became Epoptæ. The ceremonies were called Teletai, perfectings. They remained in use for 1800 years, and were only ceased in the time of the Emperor Theodosius, A.D. 395.

Mention of 9 Worthies is found in literature; they were 3 Gentiles—Hector son of King Priam, Alexander the Great and Julius Cæsar; 3 Jews—Joshua, David and Judas Maccabeus; 3 Christians—King Arthur of Britain, Charlemagne and Godfrey de Bouillon.

THE DECAD. 10.

THE Decad, number Ten, or PANTELEIA, which meant "All complete" or fully accomplished," is the grand summit of numbers, which once reached cannot be passed; to increase the sum we must retrograde to the Monad.

The Pythagoreans were entranced with its virtues and called it Deity, Heaven, Eternity and the Sun.

Ten being the recipient or receptacle of all numbers was called Decad, from *dechomai* = to receive, and hence Heaven, which was ordained to receive all men.

Like the Deity it is a Circle, with visible centre, but its circumference too vast for sight.

It is the sum of the units of the number four as previously mentioned, a holy and Deistic number, thus $4 + 3 + 2 + 1$ are 10, and thus ten gains splendour from its parentage.

Also spoken of as "Eternity," which is infinite life, because it contains every number in itself, and number is infinite.

It is also called Kosmos, that is the "Universe." Proclus says: The decad is mundane also, it is the world which receives the images of all the divine numbers, which are supernaturally imparted to it.

It is called "the fountain of eternal nature," because if we take the half, five as the middle number, and add together the next above and the next below, viz., 6 and 4, we make to, and the next two in a similar manner 7 and 3 are 10; and so on 8 and 2 and 9 and 1 give the same result.

All nations reckon by the Decimal scale of notation, to which they were no doubt led from the convenience of counting the ten digits of the hands.

It is also spoken of as *Kleidoukos*, that is, "having custody of others," the magazine of the other numbers, because other numbers are branches from it: also called Fate, which comprises all sorts of events: Age, Power; Atlas, because it supports the to spheres of Heaven; Phanes; Memory; Urania; and "The first Square, because it consists of the first four numbers."

Two old conceits were that the Tenth wave of the sea is always larger than others; and that birds laid the 10th egg of a larger size than the others.

The word Ten was used by the Hebrews, instead of "a large number," so that care must be exercised in translating this; thus Nehemiah interprets "ten generations" of Deuteronomy xxiii. v. 3 to mean "for ever." Nehemiah xiii. 1.

The Kabalists called 5, 6 and 10 circular numbers, because when squared, the result shows the same number in the unit figure, thus:

5 times 5 are 25 and 5 times 25 are 125

6 times 6 are 36   6 times 36 are 216

10 times 10 are 100   10 times 100 are 1000

An old periphrasis mentioned by Shakespeare is, "I'd set my ten commandments in your face," meaning the finger nails for scratching. See 2 Henry VI. i. 3.

The Mahometans say that ten animals were admitted to Paradise.

1. Kratim, the dog of the Seven Sleepers.

2. Ass of Balaam.

3. Ant of Solomon.

4. Whale of Jonah.

5. The Calf (not Ram) offered to Jehovah by Abraham instead of Isaac, his son.

6. The Ox of Moses.

7. The Camel of the prophet Salech.

8. The Cuckoo of Belkis.

9. The Ram of Ishmael.

10. Al Borek, the Animal which conveyed Mahomet to heaven.

"We find to generations from Adam to Noah, 10 from Shem to Abraham. The 10 spiritual graces of Christianity are Love, joy, peace, long-suffering, gentleness, goodness, faith, prudence, meekness, and temperance," says Dr. G. Oliver; although where he gets 10 generations from Adam to Noah, I know not.

Under to also falls the mention of the Pythagorean Triangle, Tetractys, consisting of an equilateral triangle enclosing ten YODS: thus the upper is the Monad, the second line the Dyad, the third the Triad, and the fourth the Quaternary or Tetrad: representing the four forms of point, line, superficies and solid. A similar form is given by Hebrew Kabalists to form 72, the deity number, by placing in a triangle four Yods, three Hehs, two Vaus and one Heh final, being the letters IHVH of the Tetragrammaton; or they may be put conversely.

Note that ten is used as a sign of fellowship, love, peace, and Union, in the Masonic third token, the union of two five points of Fellowship.

In the Bible we notice to Commandments, to instruments to which Jewish Psalms were sung, to strings in the Psaltery, and that the Holy Ghost descended ten days after the Ascension.

Tucer, Rabanus and Raymond Lully associate the numbers 8 to Air, 5 to Fire, 6 to Earth and 12 to Water.

Apuleius states that among the Egyptians it was customary to fast to days before sacrificing, and Budge says that they used a to-day week.

The Ten Sephiroth form the essence of the Hebrew dogmatic Kabalah, a subject which is too vast and complex to be entered upon in this volume on numerals. A mere glance at the Sephirotic emanations of the Absolute Deity from the mathematical point of view is all that can be attempted; my "Introduction to the Kabalah" may be referred to.

From the Absolute Passive Negativity AIN, proceeds AIN SUPH the Limitless, and then AIN SUPH AUR Boundless Light, which concentrates in the first manifestation of the Sephiroth, which is the Crown, KTR, Kether: from Kether proceeds ChKMH, Chochmah, Wisdom, an active masculine potency, and BINH, Binah, Understanding, a passive feminine power.

These three form the Supernal Triad. The fourth and fifth are ChSD, Chesed, Mercy, active and male, and GBVRH, Geburah, Strength, passive and female.

The sixth Sephira is the notable TPART, Tiphereth, Beauty, the central sun, the Logos, the Manifested Son: this completes a second triangle, the reflection of the former.

Number seven is NTZCh, Netzach, Victory, active, and the eighth is HVD, Hod, Splendour, passive; the ninth is YSVD, Yesod, the Foundation, completing the third trinity, or triangle.

MLKT, Malkuth, the Tenth Sephira, completes the emanations. She is the Bride of Microprosopus the Son, the Sun, Logos; she is the Inferior Mother, Queen, and the Manifested Universe.

The whole Ten are viewed as reigning over Four Worlds or Planes of Existence; these are the Worlds of Aziluth, Briah, Yetzirah and Assiah. Malkuth on the plane of Assiah alone is the visible tangible universe.

These Ten Sephiroth are the prototypes of everything spiritual, and also of every part of creation: they are traced in the angelic host and in our universe: three superior, and seven succedent exist in all things; the lower seven are obvious to the uninitiated, but in these manifestations the supernal triad is veiled to the profane.

Some occultists phrase it thus—three are subjective and incomprehensible to man; seven are objective and comprehensible; thus Seven archangels are commonly named, and we have known only of Seven great planets of our system.

But in some cases even the whole of seven are unknown; we acknowledge but five senses in man, but there are two more awaiting perception by process of evolution.

These Ten Sephiroth are not only viewed as triads from above below, but are also imaged in three columns entitled the Pillars of Severity and Mercy, with the median of Benignity or Mildness. But this scheme is not for this treatise, nor can the Sephirotic alliance with the Planetary symbols, the angelic host, the divine names, and the Book of Thoth, or Tarot be here described; these subjects present a mine of wisdom concealed in the rituals of the Kabalistic "Chabrath zereh aur bokher," from whose parent stem the Rosicrucian Fraternities also may have arisen. These Rituals contain a more complete scheme of the mediæval occult symbolism than exists in any other form known to me, and I believe that it would not be possible for anyone to reconstitute so complete a system out of all extant literature.

There are 10 Grades in the Rosicrucian Society; they are Zelator, Theoricus, Practicus, Philosophus; Minor, Major and Exempt Adept; Master, Magus and King: some Magi are known, but only Magi know of a Rex.

Rosicrucian private rituals give the correct names and Kabalistic spelling of the Ten heavens of the World of Assiah, which is the material universe.

H. P. Blavatsky declared that a scheme of the Zodiac of 10 Signs preceded that of 12 Signs, but I have been unable to verify the statement, by any ancient work.

Hebrew and Talmudic references are as follows:—10 men were necessary to form a legally-convened meeting at the Synagogue: in London as much as £1000 a year has been spent in providing spare men for this duty. Ten curses were pronounced against Eve; see Talmud, Eiruvin, 100. 2.

Ten things were created during the twilight of the first Sabbath eve. Consult Pesachim, 54. 1.

Ten facts proved the presence of a Supernatural Power in the Temple. Yoma, 21. 1.

The Rabbis taught that a man should divorce his wife, if for 10 years she had no offspring.

At funerals, condolences were recited by to men, and at weddings by ten men including the bridegroom. Ten cups were drunk at a funeral party—three before supper, three at supper, and four after the meal at the recitation of the four blessings.

Abraham was tested to times; to Miracles were performed in Egypt to help the Children of Israel, and to at the Red Sea. Ten plagues were made to afflict the Egyptians. Ten times the Jews offended God in the Wilderness.

Ten times did the Shekinah come down into the world; at the Garden of Eden; at the Tower of Babel; at Sodom; in Egypt, see Exodus iii. 8; at the Red Sea, Psalm cviii. 9; on Mount Sinai; at the Temple; in the Pillar of Cloud; on the Mount of Olives, see Zechariah xiv. 4; the 10th is omitted in the original reference, Avoth d' Rabbi Nathan, chap. 34.

There are to Hebrew words to designate Idols, and to for Joy. Sodom was to be spared for to righteous men; Gideon took to servants to destroy the Altar of Baal; Boaz chose to witnesses for his marriage with Ruth; Joab's armour was borne by to young men. Jesus speaks of 10 talents, 10 cities, 10 pieces of silver, and gave a parable of to Virgins. The Tabernacle has many to dimensions. There are to Bible names of God, to Canticles, and to necessaries for man's life. Ecclus. 39. 26.

There were to Pythagorean Virtues of Initiation, and the Buddhists teach to Paramitas of Perfection.

In the Alchymico-Kabalistic tract called "Aesch Metzareph" referred to by Eliphaz Levi, and collected from the Zohar of Knorr von Rosenroth and translated into English, and forming Volume IV. of my "Collectanea Hermetica," will be found 10 names for Gold all extracted from the Old Testament; they are there related to the Sephira Geburah.

The Hindoo Puranas tell us of the 10 Avatars of the God Vishnu, the Preserver of the Brahmanic Religion; they are periodical incarnations of the God. First as the Fish, Matsya; 2. Kurma, the Tortoise; 3. Varaha, the Boar; 4. Narasingha, the Man-Lion; 5. Vamana, the Dwarf; 6. Parasu-Rama; 7. Rama Chandra; 8. Krishna; 9. Buddha; and the 10th, Kalki, the Horse, is yet to come. These Avatars are susceptible of a mystical explanation on the plane of cosmogony; it has been given in the Garuda Temple of the "Oriental Order of Light" by Frater T. H. Pattinson of Bradford, a very notable mystic and occult student.

In the Yoga Vasishtha Maha Ramayana of Valmiki, edited by Vihari Lala Mitra, will be found an essay on Om-Tat-Sat, on-id-est, and this contains some very curious information on the to numerals as related to the mystical syllable Om or AUM.

"Aum mani padmé hum" means literally, "Oh, the jewel in the lotus," and is taken mystically to mean "the spark of the Divine within me," as was fully explained by Blavatsky to her Esoteric section of Theosophists.

ELEVEN. 11.

THIS seems to have been the type of a number with an evil reputation among all peoples. The Kabalists contrasted it with the perfection of the Decad, and just as the Sephirotic number is the form of all good things, so eleven is the essence of all that is sinful, harmful and imperfect; with the Ten Sephiroth they contrasted the Eleven Averse Sephiroth, symbols of destruction, violence, defeat and death. On the oldest Tarot cards, the trump called the Tower struck by Lightning, number XVI, shows the Ten Divine Sephiroth on one side and the Eleven Averse Sephiroth on the other side; modern Tarot designs are very much debased.

John Heydon says that by it we know the bodies of Devils and their nature; the Jews understand by it Lilith, Adam's first wife, a she-devil, dangerous to women in confinements; hence they wrote on the walls:—ADM ChVH ChVO LILIT, that is, Adam, Eve, out of doors Lilith."

Jesus, in Matt. xii. 43, plainly allows the doctrine that evil spirits may haunt fields, which Grotius says the Jews think; and their word Demon and Field are similar, being ShDIM (fields), and ShDIM (evil deities); the Siddim are mentioned in Psalm cvi. 37.

It is called the "Number of Sins" and the "Penitent," because it exceeds the number of the Commandments, and is less than twelve, which is the number of Grace and Perfection. But sometimes even eleven receives a favour from God, as in the case of the man who was called in the eleventh hour to the vineyard, who yet received the same pay as the others.

Rabbi Jochanan says that eleven sorts of spices were mentioned by God to Moses on Mount Sinai as suitable for holy incense.

Eleven was the number of the Disciples of Jesus, after the fall of Judas Iscariot.

In the Hebrew Language the word eleven was expressed as Achad Osher, AI, or One and Ten.

TWELVE. 12.

THIS number has a perfect and notable character, and was highly esteemed by most nations of antiquity. Almost all the twelves will be found to be allied, either obviously or in a concealed manner, with the Signs of the Zodiac, twelve signs or partitions of the great circle of the heavens—twelve times thirty degrees forming the perfect cycle of 360 arithmetical degrees of the circle: each sign was further sub-divided into three decans. There are many of the learned who believe the twelve sons of Jacob, and twelve founders of tribes, are allegorical only. We may mention the "Twelve Grand Points of Masonry," which used to form a part of the lectures in the Craft degrees. Twelve events in the ceremony of initiation, referred to the sons of Jacob, are given by Mackey:

1. To Reuben was referred the opening of the Lodge—he was the first-born son.

2. To Simeon, the preparation of the land—he prepared the destruction of the Shechemites.

3. To Levi, the report or signal—he gave the signal in the attack on the men of Shechem.

4. To Judah, the entrance of the land—that tribe first entered the promised land.

5. To Zebulun, the prayer—the prayer and blessing of his father fell on him in preference to Issachar.

6. To Issachar, the circumambulation—an indolent tribe, who required a leader.

7. To Dan, the advance to the Altar—for a contrast to their rapid advance to idolatry.

8. To Gad, the obligation—on account of Jephthah's vow.

9. To Asher, the entrusting; with rich Masonic blessings—resembled the Fathers of their land.

10. To Naphtali, the investment and declared "Free"—the tribe of Naphtali had a peculiar freedom given by Moses.

11. To Joseph, the N.E. corner—because Ephraim and Manasseh (grandsons) represented him, newest corners.

12. To Benjamin, the closing of the Lodge—as being the last son of the Patriarch.

The following associations of Birds, Animals, and Flowers with heavenly bodies has the authority of the Greco-Roman mythology:—

Greek.	Latin.	Bird.	Animal.	Vegetable.
Pallas	Minerva	Owl	She-goat	Olive
Aphrodite	Venus	Dove	He-goat	Myrtle
Helios	Sol	Cock	Bull	Laurel
Hermes	Mercury	Ibis	Dog	Hazel
Zeus	Jupiter	Eagle	Hart	Horse-chestnut.
Demeter	Ceres	Sparrow	Sow	Apple

Hephaistos	Vulcan	Goose	Ass	Box
Ares	Mars	Magpie	Wolf	Dog-wood
Artemis	Diana	Daw	Hind	Palm
Hestia	Vesta	Heron	Lion	Pine
Hera	Juno	Peacock	Sheep	Thorn
Poseidon	Neptune	Swan	Horse	Elm

The astrologers associated colours with the twelve Signs of the Zodiac, thus:—

With Pisces, white

,, Aquarius, blue

,, Capricorn, black or brown

,, Sagittarius, yellow or green

,, Scorpio, brown

,, Libra, black or crimson

,, Virgo, black and blue

With Leo, red and green

,, Cancer, green and brown

,, Gemini, red

,, Aries, white

,, Taurus, white and yellow

The Zodiacal Signs are also associated with Sex, and the contrast of Day and Night.

Pisces	Female	Nocturnal
Aquarius	Male	Diurnal
Capricorn	Female	Nocturnal
Sagittarius	Male	Diurnal
Scorpio	Female	Nocturnal
Libra	Male	Diurnal
Virgo	Female	Nocturnal
Leo	Male	Diurnal
Cancer	Female	Nocturnal
Gemini	Male	Diurnal
Taurus	Female	Nocturnal
Aries	Male	Diurnal

And, again, there are other characters which astrologers deem of importance, thus:—

Pisces	Water	Northern	Common	Fruitful
Aquarius	Air	Western	Fixed	
Capricorn	Earth	Southern	Cardinal	
Sagittarius	Fire	Eastern	Common	
Scorpio	Water	Northern	Fixed	Fruitful
Libra	Air	Western	Cardinal	
Virgo	Earth	Southern	Common	Barren

Leo	Fire	Eastern	Fixed	Barren
Cancer	Water	Northern	Cardinal	Fruitful
Gemini	Air	Western	Common	Barren
'Taurus	Earth	Southern	Fixed	
Aries	Fire	Eastern	Cardinal	

Lastly, the twelve signs are allotted to the planets as their houses:—

Pisces—the night house of Jupiter

Aquarius—the day house of Saturn (Uranus)

Capricorn—the night house of Saturn

Sagittarius—the night house of Mars

Libra—the day house of Venus

Virgo—the night house of Mercury

Leo—the sole house of Sol

Cancer—the sole house of Luna

Gemini—the day house of Mercury

Taurus—the night house of Venus

Aries—the day house of Mars.

This is very fully explained by Coley in his "Astrology," and also by John Middleton in his "Astrology," 1679.

Herodotus tells us that the Egyptians founded the system of a Twelve-God theology: Euterpe iv. The Hebrews certainly at times worshipped the Sun, Moon, seven planets, and the Star Rulers of the Twelve Zodiacal Signs: see 2 Kings xxiii. 5, and Job xxxviii. 32. Dunlop, in his "Vestiges," remarks that of the names of the twelve months in use among the Jews, several are identical with names of Deities, as Tammuz, Ab, Elul, Bul. Groups of twelve Gods are to be noticed in the religions of many of the ancient nations, as the Chaldeans, Etruscans, Mamertines, Romans, etc.

In Scandinavia the Great Odin had 12 names—personified attributes.

The Kabalists esteem the 12 permutations of the Tetragrammaton, IHVH, VHIH, HIHV, HVHI, IHHV, IVHH, HVIH, VIHH, HHVI, HHIV, HIVH, VHHI.

The Talmuds say:—

No deceased person is at heart lost to his relatives until after 12 months; see the Treatise Berachoth.

How was the Witch of Endor able to bring up Samuel by necromancy? To this question Rabbi Abhu answered, because he had not been dead 12 months: after that time it would not have been possible, for then the body is destroyed and the Soul has gone up into the next world.

The Rabbis said that at the first revelation the True Name of God was a word of 12 letters. Kiddushin, 71. 1.

The Mishna narrates the events of the first 12 hours; Adam fell into sin in the tenth Hour, was judged in the eleventh, and was cast out of the Garden in the twelfth; so he abode not even one day in his dignity. Sanhedrin, 38. 2. Compare the "Nuctemeron" of Apollonius of Tyana, given by Eliphaz Lévi in his "Rituel de la Magie," Paris, 1861.

The 12 Stones of the High Priest's Breast-plate were named;—Sardius, Topaz, Carbuncle, Emerald, Sapphire, Diamond, Ligure or Jacinth, Agate, Amethyst, Beryl, Onyx, and Jasper. See Hebrew Ancient Version, Exodus xxviii.

The 12 Foundations of the Heavenly City, given in Revelations xxi., are,—Jasper, Sapphire, Chalcedony, Sardius, Sardonyx, Emerald, Topaz, Beryl, Chrysolite, Amethyst, Jacinth and Chrysophrasus.

The 12 Hebrew Months were Abib or Nizan (March–April), Iyar or Zif, Sivan, Thammuz, Ab, Elul, Tisri, Bul, Chisleu, Tebeth, Shebat, Adar; and the inter-calary month Ve-Adar.

The 12 Egyptian Months were Pachon, Paoni, Epiphi, Mesori, Thoth, Phaophi, Athyr, Choiak, Tobi, Mechir, Phamenoth and Pharmuthi; the last beginning on March 27th.

The 12 Sons of Jacob were related to the 12 Signs of the Zodiac by the Rosicrucians in a correct order; other schemes of attribution are given by Athanasius Kircher and others.

That by Sir William Drummond is:—Aries to Gad, Taurus to Ephraim, Gemini to Benjamin, Cancer to Issachar, Leo to Judah, Virgo to Naphtali, Libra to Asher, Scorpio to Dan, Sagittary to Manasseh, Capricorn to Zebulun, Aquarius to Reuben, and Pisces to Simeon and Levi.

The 12 Apostles of Jesus were;—Simon Peter, Andrew, James and John the sons of Zebedee, Philip, Bartholomew, Thomas, Matthew also called Levi, James son of Alphæus, Judas called Lebbæus and Thaddeus, Simon the Canaanite, and Judas Iscariot. The Venerable Bede proposed to rename the Signs with the names of the apostles, and a scheme of allotment is to be found in "The Sphere of Marcus Manilius," by Edward Sherburne, London, 1675. See "Notes and Queries," Vol. xiv., Manchester, U.S.A., p. 211. Westcott on the Zodiac in Soc. Ros. Reports gives the Christian allusions to the Zodiac.

In an ordinary pack of Playing Cards there are 12 Court Cards, but in the Tarot Pack there are also 4 Cavaliers.

The Kabalists greatly esteemed the 12-lettered Name of God, HIH-HVVH-VIHIH, meaning "fuit, est, erit,"—or,—He was, is, will be.

Less esoteric was the Triple Tetragrammaton, IHVH thrice written.

All Fratres of the Rosicrucian Society of England will also be familiar with AB BEN V Ruch H QDSh, Ab-Ben-ve-Ruach-ha-Kodesh; meaning Father, Son and Holy Spirit.

The Rosicrucian Society had a scheme of distributing 12 shades of Colour among the Zodiacal Signs, but this is a secret matter; many erroneous schemes have been published.

The 12 Signs of the Zodiac are named in Hebrew, beginning with Aries; Taleh, Shur, Thaumim, Sartan, Ariah, Bethuleh, Mazanaim, Akrab, Kesith, Gedi, Deli, and Dagim. In Arabic; Al Hamal, Al Thaur, Al Tauman, Al Sartan, Al Asad, Sunbul, Al Zubena, Al Akrab, Al Kaus, Al Gedi, Debi and Al Haut. In Chinese, Pe yaugh, the sheep; Kin nieu, golden bull; Shang huing, two brothers; Kin hiai, crab; Sin, lion; Sha niu, the house girl; Tien tchingh, the claws of a scorpion; Tien Kie, the scorpion; Gun Ma, the man horse; Mu Thien, the hill sheep; Pao pingh, precious vase; and Shang Yu, two fishes.

The old Sanskrit Hindoo names used by astrologers at the present time are; Mesha, Rishaba, Mithuna, Katakam, Simha, Kanya, Tulam, Vrishchika, Dhanus, Makaram, Kumbha and Minam.

The 12 simple letters of the Hebrew Alphabet have affinities with the Zodiacal Signs, but the order of relation is a Rosicrucian private doctrine.

There were 12 recorded Appearances of Jesus after his death; to Mary Magdalene, to the Galician women, to two disciples, to Peter, to ten apostles, to eleven apostles, to seven apostles and others when fishing, to 500 brethren at once, to James the Less, to eleven apostles, to Stephen at his martyrdom, to Paul at his Conversion, and to the apostle John.

The 12 hours marked in a watch face can be used to find the cardinal points, if the time is correct, and the sun is visible. Lay the watch flat and point the hour hand to the sun, and then the south will be half way between that hour and the figure XII.

The author of the Hymns of Orpheus, the Scholiast on Hesiod, and Porphyry state that the 12 Labours of Hercules are said to be emblems of the sun in its passage through the 12 signs, and this is repeated by the "Mystagogus Poeticus," 1653, and they have been allotted as follows:— to Aries, the quest of the Golden Apples of the Hesperides; to Taurus, the slaying of the Cretan Bull; Gemini, Hercules and his twin brother strangle the serpents; Cancer, the taking of the Herds of Geryon; Leo, the slaying of the Nemæan Lion; Virgo, the victory over the Amazon Queen; Libra, the death of the Erymanthean boar; Scorpio, the death of the Lernæan Hydra; Sagittarius, the shooting of the Stymphalian Birds; Capricornus, taking of the hind alive to Mycenæ; Aquarius, cleaning the stables of Augeas; Pisces, the capture of the horses of Diomedes.

Janus of the Romans is the God of the 12 months, and is drawn with 12 altars beneath his feet. He is the same as Assyrian Ain, Ion, Jan; ON of Eastern nations (Dunlop's "Vestiges," 31).

John Heydon gives the following statements:—

Prosperous numbers are 1 2 3 4 7 9 11 13 14

Very good „ 16 17 19 20 22 23 10 26 27

Indifferent „ 5 6 8 12 15 18 21

Very bad „ 24 25 28 29 30

THIRTEEN. 13.

THIRTEEN was the sacred number of the Mexicans and people of Yucatan: twelve of many tribes of North American Indians, as of so many nations of antiquity: this had an astronomical connection, because the Stars and Sun were Gods to them. The method of computation among the Mexican Priests was by weeks of 13 days; consult Dunlop's "Vestiges." Their year contained 28 weeks of 13 days and 1 day over, just as ours contains 52 of 7 days and one day over. Thirteen years formed an Indiction, a week of years, the 13 days over forming another week. Four times 13, or 52, years was their cycle. In Yucatan there were 13 "Snake Gods" (see Steven's "Yucatan," and Gama's "Ancient Mexicans ").

13 is the number of the Hebrew word AHBH, Ahebah, love, and of Achad, AChD, unity. Old authors state that 13 is a number used to procure agreement among married people. Hebrew ancient lore did not reckon the number 13 as unlucky; this idea arose from the fate of Judas after the Last Supper of Jesus, yet not for some centuries, but since the notion was started it has been prevalent among all Christians.

The 13 cards of each suit of a pack of Cards are sometimes applied to the 13 lunar months for purposes of divination.

The Gnostic gems are often inscribed with a 13-lettered Name for God, ABLANA Th ANALBA.

Rabbi Eliezer on account of a serious drought proclaimed 13 fasts, at the end of which rain fell at once.

The Temple used 13 collecting horns; and in it were 13 tables, and 13 devotional reverential bows were used in the full service.

When a Hebrew boy reached the age of 13 years he began to fast for the full time: a girl began at twelve years.

The word Covenant is written 13 times in the chapter on Circumcision.

The Bava Metzia gives 13 reasons for a good breakfast. In the Hebrew Liturgy are found the 13 logical rules for interpreting the law. Hershon, "Talmud Miscellany," p. 167.

SOME HINDOO USES OF NUMBERS.

IN ancient India, in the Sanscrit language, certain words were used as equivalent to the low numbers: for One they said Moon or Earth: for Two they used many words of things in pairs such as eye, wing, arm: for Three they used Rama, fire or guna, for they knew of 3 Ramas, 3 kinds of fire and 3 gunas or qualities: for 4 they used Veda, age or ocean: for 6 they used Seasons: for 7 they used Sage or vowel: for 12 they said Sun or Zodiac; and for 20 they used nails, meaning those of hands and feet. Edward B. Tylor.

OTHER HIGHER NUMBERS.

THE 14 days of Burial, in the Master's degree: 14 parts into which the body of Osiris was divided: a type of Christ, sacrificed on the 14th day of the month: an amulet of 14 points has been used to cure the sick.

There are 14 Books of the Apocrypha; they were written originally in Greek, never in Hebrew. An Israelite had to partake of 14 meals in the Booth during the Feast of Tabernacles.

The Israelites killed the Paschal Lamb on the 14th day of the Month Nisan.

In Matthew, chap. i., we find the genealogy of Jesus recited in three series of 14 names, the first under Patriarchs and judges, the second under kings, and the third under priests and governors.

The ancient physicians considered that the 14th day was the crisis of fevers.

The Moon waxes and wanes, each for 14 days.

15 was the number of Pairs of The Æons, or Holy Principles in the Gnostic scheme of Valentinus.

15 is the number by Gematria of the 8th Sephira Hod, HUD.

There were 15 steps in the Temple between the ante-court of Israel and the Women's Court, and in these were sung the 15 Psalms of Degrees; Psalms cxx.–cxxxiv. 15 is the number of Jah, a name of God; so the Jews who wrote letters for numbers, never wrote JH, 10, 5, for 15, but TV, 9, 6 15.

The great day of joyful recreation for Jewish Maidens was the 15th day of the month Ab. The Deluge covered the hills to the depth of 15 cubits.

A Jewish boy in the olden time was ordered to begin the study of the Gemara when 15 years of age.

16 means Felicity; a square number. There are 16 Court Cards in a Tarot pack.

17. In the treatise "De Iside et Osiride," Plutarch says Osiris was killed on the 17th day of the moon, and hence when the moon was at the full—and from that reason the Egyptians abominate the number 17, and so did the Pythagoreans—they called in Antiphraxis (obstruction), because it falls between the square number 16 and the oblong number 18.

18 was deemed a protection against thieves.

18. Isaiah made 18 denunciations against Israel. At 18 years of age a girl should go to the Nuptial Canopy. The Golden Candlestick of the Temple was 18 hands-breadths tall. There are 18 Blessings in the Hebrew Liturgy. There were only 18 High Priests during the existence of the First or Solomonic Temple at Jerusalem.

19. The number 19 is famous as being the number of years in the Metonic Cycle; the cycle of the revolutions of the moon, after which she returns to have her changes on the same day of the solar year. Meto lived 433 B.C.; he was an Athenian; he published his discovery at the Olympic Games in the above year. The exact period is, however, 18 years and to days. The Calippic period of four cycles, or seventy-six years, was invented by Calippus, B.C. 330, to correct Meto. John Heydon says that the number 19 facilitates births and menses.

20. The Kiddushin, 29. 2, says God may curse a man who does not marry at least when 20 years old, for his life is a constant transgression. A woman marrying before 20 may bear children up to sixty; at 20 until forty, and after forty will have none. Bava Bathra, 119. 2. To die after 20 days' diarrhœa is to die pure.

21. A hen sits 21 days, and the Almond is ripe 21 days after the flower falls.

22 Letters of the Hebrew Alphabet, used also as numerals. The realization of a good Dream may be deferred 22 years. Berachoth, 55. 2.

From the Works of Hermes Trismegistus are abstracted 22 axioms on the Human Will; they can be found in Tukaram Tatya's "Guide to Theosophy," Bombay, 1887.

There are 22 Trumps in a pack of ancient Tarot Cards, used for Divination; Eliphaz Lévi, in his "Clef des Mystères," says that the numbers 1 to 19 refer to the Keys of Occult Science, and that numbers 19 to 22 are the Keys of Nature: the relation of letters to these are nowhere correctly printed in books.

23. In the Sanhedrin 23 judges were required to try cases punishable by death.

23. This day of September is notable because the moon which comes to the full within a fortnight of it is called the harvest moon, which rises three days in succession at the same time, instead of getting daily later.

24 is an evil number, referring to Cain, QIN, but not of his numeration, which is $100 + 10 + 50 = 160$, or else $100 + 10 + 700 = 810$.

24. There are 24 birds unclean as food; 24 ribs both in man and woman.

26. The number of Jehovah, IHVH, $10 + 5 + 6 + 5$.

26. In the English language, which uses 26 letters, it is found that the letters occur in very different proportions. In a fair example of modern English it has been calculated that the proportion between the frequency of the use of the letters was, of a, 85; b, 16; c, 30; d, 44; e, 120; f, 25; g, 17; h, 64; i, 80; j, 4; k, 8; l, 40; m, 30; n, 80; o, 80; p, 17; q, 5; r, 62; s, 80; t, 90; u, 34; v, 12; w, 20; x, 4; y, 20; and z, 2.

27. The number of the Izeds or Angels who ruled under the supervision of the Seven Amshaspands of the Zoroastrian theology.

28. A division of the Zodiac into 28 mansions of the moon, was probably earlier than the solar division into 12 parts. The names and symbols can be obtained in Sanskrit and in Arabic. Proctor believes that Solar Astronomy of the 12 signs arose about 2170 B.C., in a country of about 36 degrees of north latitude, and at a period when Taurus was the first constellation of the Zodiac.

29. The Rosh Hashanha says the period of the Moon's Revolution is 29 days and six hours and forty minutes.

30. A meal of Lentils once in 30 days keeps off the Quinsy. At 30 years of age Jesus began his ministry; Joseph was 30 years old when he stood before Pharaoh; David was 30 years old when he began to reign; 30 pieces of silver was the price Judas received, and Jair had 30 sons.

31. The number of El, God = AL. 1 + 30.

31. Joshua did not complete the conquest of Canaan until he had slain 31 kings.

32. The number of the Paths of Wisdom, of the Sepher Yetzirah, being Io Sephiroth and 22 letters of the Hebrew alphabet.

33. The years of the life of Jesus: King David reigned in Jerusalem 33 years: the number of vertebræ in the human spinal column.

35. The number of Agla, AGLA, a composite Kabalistic wonder-working name. See page 27.

36. Abaji said there are never less than 36 holy men of any generation upon whom the Shekinah does not rest.

36. Plutarch, "De Iside et Osiride," calls the Tetractys the power of the number 36, and on this was the greatest oath of the Pythagoreans sworn; and it was denominated the World, in consequence of its being composed of the first four even and the first four odd numbers; for 1 and 3 and 5 and 7 are 16; add 2 and 4 and 6 and 8, and obtain 36.

39. The number of Articles of the Protestant Christian Church belief.

40. Up to 40 years of age eating is best for a man, after 40 drinking suits best. He who has passed 40 days without an affliction has had his reward in this life.

For 40 days the Flood lasted, for 40 days the spies searched the promised land, for 40 days Goliath challenged Israel, 40 days of Ezekiel's penitence, the Jews were 40 years in the Wilderness, 40 days of waiting before embalming the dead, Genesis 1. 3; for 40 days the woman's purification lasted after childbirth; for 40 days Moses fasted twice; for 40 days Elijah fasted, and for 40 days Jesus fasted in the Wilderness, and 40 days elapsed between the Resurrection and Ascension of Jesus. Moses was 40 years in Egypt, 40 in Midian, and 40 in the Wilderness. The Israelites were 40 years among the Philistines.

42 is notable because of the 42-lettered name of God, taught by the Kabalists: there were 42 Judges in the Judgment Hall of Osiris. See Bettany, "The World's Religions," p. 166, on the events of the 42nd day after death.

42. The Talmud of Babylon in Kiddushin 71, mentions the 42-lettered Name, and it is given by Ignatz Stern as composed of the Divine Names of the Bible; thus Eheieh asher eheieh, Al, Jah, Jehovah, Elohim, Jehovah Sabaoth, El Chai and Adonai. AHIH AShR AHIH; IH; IHVIH; AL; ALHIM; IHVH TzBAVT; AL ChI; ADNI, Or 4, 3, 4, 2, 5, 2, 5, 4, 5, 2, 2, 4 = 42.

It is very curious that the Ten Sephiroth which denote the attributes of God will show, when these letters are added together, and a V added for *and* before the last one, this same number 42; if Chesed be called Gedulah, as was common among Kabalists.

45. The number of Adam, ADM.

45. The world is preserved for the sake of 45 righteous persons. Chullin, 92.

48. There have been 48 prophets in Israel: 48 cities were assigned to the Levites.

49. Moses received 49 reasons for the cleanness and uncleanness of each thing: so says The Talmud.

50. The number of the Gates of Binah (BINH) the Understanding. The Kabalah states that even Moses only reached the 49th. See my "Sepher Yetzirah," Third Edition, 1911.

58. Noah, Nch.

60. Aristotle stated that the Crocodile lives naturally 60 years, and sits 60 days on 60 eggs.

The Chinese have a time cycle of 60 years, and call it Kya-tse. The people of Malabar call this period Chi-tam.

60. The Talmud refers to 60 deadly drugs, and 60 sorts of wines; the sow bears her litter in 60 days.

6i. The number AIN, Negative existence of the Deity.

64. Aletheia, truth.

65. The number of Adonai, translated "Lord" (ADNI) and of Hs, Hes, keep silence.

67. The number of Binah, Supernal Mother, the 3rd Sephira.

70. The number of SUD, Sod, a secret doctrine and private assembly: the earliest name for the Kabalah: also IIN, Yayin, wine, also meant a secret.

70. The Rabbis considered that there were 70 nations, and Mordecai is said to have known 70 languages. The Jewish 70 years of the captivity are reckoned from their conquest by Nebuchadnezzar to the accession of Cyrus.

71. The number of the Members of the Sanhedrin.

72 has a large number of mystic references—to the 72 angels bearing the names of God—derived from Exodus xiv. 19, 20, 21, by the Kabalists; there is an important set of 72 pentacles which, placed in pairs, forms a series of 36 talismans (see Dr. Rudd, the Lemegeton, Harleian MSS.); it is also the number of Chesed (ChSD) the Sephira, Mercy.

72. It is said that Ptolemy, King of Egypt, collected 72 Hebrew Rabbis and confined each in a separate room, and ordered each to write out the Mosaic Law, and that by the help of God each wrote out the same words. Megillah of the Talmud, 9. 1.

This account is similar to that of Josephus and Aristæus, but different to that of Philo: hence the name Septuagint.

73. The number of Chokmah (ChKMH), Wisdom, the 2nd Sephira.

78. The number of cards in a Tarot pack: 40 numerals, r6 court cards and 22 Trumps.

79. Boz, Boaz, the left-hand brazen Pillar at the entrance to Solomon's Temple.

80. The number of Yesod, foundation, 9th Sephira. 80. The venerable Rabbi Hillel had 80 pupils.

81. According to the Book of Rites of Chao Kung, B.C. 1112, an Emperor of China should have 3 concubines of the First rank, 9 of the Second, 27 of the Third and 81 of the Fourth Rank.

90. IKIN, Jachin, the right-hand Pillar of Solomon's Temple.

91 is the number of AMN and of Tetragrammaton Adonai (IHVH, ADNI).

96. According to Vitruvius the natural height of a typical adult man is 96 digits, which equalled 24 palms, or six feet.

99. The Mahometans have 99 names attributed to God.

100. This is the number of MDVN, which means strife, and it is the beginning of 100 lawsuits.

The Jerusalem Talmud, Bava Metzia, 85. 1, says that Rabbi Zira fasted 100 times to enable him to forget the Talmud of Babylon, in favour of the Talmud of Jerusalem.

Obadiah was considered worthy to be called prophet, because he concealed 100 prophets in a cave.

103. The family of Herod Asmonæus ruled Jewry 103 years.

120. For 120 years the secret vault of Christian Rosenkreutz remained unopened, as he had ordered, 1484 to 1604.

The Shemaneh Esreh, the 18 Blessings, were composed by 120 Elders.

130. The Rabbis said that after the curse Adam fasted 130 years as a penance. This number is referred to Elijah, ALIHV, and to the word prophet, HNBIA; these names number 120, add 10 to this, the number of letters. The Kabalists make a Mystical Square (rectangle) or Kamea of ALIHV of 130 permutations; ten by thirteen.

152. The number of Maria, the Greek name for Mary the Virgin, being 40, 1, 100, 10, 1 =152.

153. The number of the great fishes caught in an unbroken net by the Apostles after the Resurrection.

200. The number of the bones in the human body.

207. This is the number of Ain Suph, AIN SVP, the Boundless, and Aur, AVR, Light, and of Adonai Olam, ADNI OVLAM, Lord of the Universe.

216. The cube of 6; 216 years, the period of the Pythagorean Metempsychosis.

221. The Cup of David in heaven contains 221 logs of wine: (about 20 gallons) says the Talmud.

231. The sum of the numbers 1 to 21, the Gates of the Sepher Yetzirah.

243. Circles of Zoir Anpin; the number of the permutations, without reversal of the Hebrew Letters. Kalisch.

248. There are 248 members of the body, says Talmud Eiruvin, 53. 2, and an anathema enters into all of them. The word ChRM, accursed, is 248, but so is RChM, Mercy.

252. It is said that the disciples of Rabbi Ishmael once dissected a low woman, and found she had 252 members; but it does not say what the extra ones were.

270. Worlds of the Idra Rabba, or Greater Holy Assembly.

271. The Talmud, in Niddah, says that the Hebrew woman's pregnancy lasted 271, 272 or 273 days.

280 days the term of natural pregnancy, human;-ten times the Lunar 28 day period.

284. The number of Theos, God, in Greek letters.

294. Ekklesia, The Church and RODON, the Rose, and also Melchisedek, King of Salem.

300. Mithras.

300. The riches of Korah were so vast that it took 300 mules to carry them.

There were 300 sorts of devils in Sichin.

The Veil of the Temple required 300 priests to draw it aside, and 300 to cleanse it.

314. The number of Shaddai, ShDI and of Metatron, MTTRUN.

318. Helios, the Sun.

345. This is the number of El Shaddai, AL ShDI, God Almighty; and of ShMH (Shemah), the Name of the Absolute God: also of MShH, Moses, and ShILH, Shiloh.

358. The number of Messiah, Mshich and Nchsh nachash, the Serpent symbol of life.

364. The name Satan, the Shathan, H,shThN, contains 364, and all these days of each year he can tempt man, but not on the 365th, the Day of Atonement.

365. The Greek numeration of Abraxas, a Gnostic talismanic word.

365. Days of the year, Negative Jewish precepts, Dukes of Babylon, and Streets in the City of Rome.

370. Directions of the thought of Microprosopus. See Idra Rabba, 5. 537.

373. Logos.

375. ShLMH, Solomon.

394. There were this number of law-courts in the Jerusalem of the kingdom period.

400. The body of Joseph was carried 400 miles to burial. David is said to have had a guard of 400 young men who rode in golden chariots at the head of his army.

410. The First Temple stood ¢lo years, and the Second Temple 420.

474. The number of Daath, DOT, Secret Wisdom, the union of Chokmah and Binah.

496. The number of Malkuth (MLKT), the Kingdom, the 10th Sephira.

500. Kosmos.

543. The number of the mystic name Aheie asher Aheie, "I am that I am" (AHIH AShR AHIH).

550. ShMIR, the Shamir, the magical insect which cut the stones for Solomon's Temple.

608 is a very notable number, representing the Sun. Martianus Capella, of the 5th century, says: "The Sun is called in Italy the 'God Sol'; at the Nile, Serapis; at Memphis, Osiris; he is also Attis; Adonis at Byblos; and Ammon in Libya; also Typhon, Mithras, and Pluto; his holy name is of 3 letters, which number 608." In Chaldee and Hebrew 608 is Cham, or Ham (ChM), which also means, "heat." In Greek Y.H.S. from U.H.S. = 400 + 8 + 200 = 608. Tyre, TRCh, is also an example of 608.

612. Zeus.

613. The words Moses our Rabbi, MShH RBINU; and Lord God of Israel, IHVH ALHI IshRL both number by Gematria 613. The 613 Precepts of the Jewish law were delivered to Moses. David, it is said, reduced them to eleven, and Isaiah to six, and later to two. Habakkuk to One, viz., The just shall live by Faith. 613 also refers to the holy garment which had 600 fringes, eight threads and five knots.

620. The number of Kether, KTR, the Crown, or 1st Sephira.

622 years from the Christian era is the date of the Hegira, or flight of Mahomet from Mecca, from which year the Mahometans reckon their calendar.

632 years A.D. is the foundation of the Persian mode of reckoning years, from their king Yezdegird.

640 is Shemesh, the Sun, ShMSh; Mem is water; place the three letters one above the other, and we get Sh, fire, sun, rising above and sinking below the waters.

646. The total numeration of Elohim, or Aleim ALHIM, being 1 + 30 + 5 + 10 + 600; or avoiding the use of final Mem, we get 1 + 30 + 5 + 10 + 40; neglecting the tens 1 + 3 + 5 + 1 + 4, and placing these figures in a circle, we get the sequence 3.1415, notable as the value of π,

or the relation of a diameter to circumference of every circle. Elohim is both a singular and a plural word.

650 has been referred by Godfrey Higgins to Noah, Menes, and Bacchus. Noah, in Hebrew, is NVCh or 64.

651 Teletai, the Greek Ancient Mysteries and Epistëmë—Science.

666 is the pet number of Godfrey Higgins, as referred to Rasit (RSVT), 200 + 60 + 6 + 400, which he insists means Wisdom—or as most believe—Beginning or Principle: The first words of Genesis are be-rasit, In the beginning.

666. The number of the Beast, the number of a Man, has been associated with Satan, Mahomet, the Pope and a hundred others. It is also the number of SVRT, the Hebrew word for the Sun. It occurs in Revelations xiii. 18.

666 is also the diameter of a circle whose circumference is 2093, which is the diagonal of a square whose sides are 1480, the number of Christos. It is also the sum of the numbers 1 to 36. It is also the number of Syënë in Greek, a place in Egypt at which, if a pit be dug, said Eratosthenes, the rays of the Sun at the Summer Solstice shine perpendicularly into it.

700. The Talmud says there are 700 species of fishes, and in Eiruvin, 18. 1, it says that God plaited Eve's hair into 700 braids.

753 B.C. The founding of the City of Rome.

753. The number alike of Abram with Sarai 243 and 510, and of Abraham with Sarah 248 and 505, the change which led to parenthood.

780. Ophis—serpent, and Sophia—wisdom.

Sol is the number of alpha and omega, 1 + 800, the Peristera or Dove, vehicle of the Holy Ghost; being 80 + 5 + 100 + 10 + 200 + 300 + 5 + 100 + 1 =801.

813 is the numeration of ARARITA, a very important Kabalistic word, its letters being collected from the initials of the sentence, "One principle of his unity, one beginning of his individuality, his vicissitude is one," or so it is rendered by S. L. Mathers.

831. Puramis, a pyramid and Phallos.

888. The number of Iesous, Jesus, the great contrast with 666, the number of the Beast.

891. Uranus, ουρανος—Heaven.

903. The Talmud in Berachoth, 8. 1, says that there are 903 kinds of Death, for by Gematria of the word TUTZAUT, which means "outlets" see Psalm lxviii. 20; this number is obtained, thus T, 400: V, 6: Tz, 90: A, 1: V, 6: T, 400 = 903. Death by the Divine kiss is the Euthanasia; death from quinsy is said to be the worst form, a sort of suffocation long drawn out.

950. According to Genesis ix. v. 29 Noah lived 950 years. The great ages given in the book of Genesis to the patriarchs have long been a cause of doubt: recent researches by a Hebrew scholar have led to the opinion that these high numbers did not mean our solar years, but years

of five months of thirty days, and perhaps the earliest year was only one month. David spoke of 70 years as the length of human life; there was no such long period between Noah and David as could reduce human life by eleven-twelfths.

974. There were this number of generations from the writing of the Law by the Holy One before he created Man in the World.

999. At the Judgment, although there be 999 who condemn a man, he shall be saved if One plead for him.

1000. The 1000-headed serpent is Sesha or Ananta, the Hindoo emblem of eternity.

1000. The daughter of Pharaoh, whom Solomon married, told him of 1000 forms of musical instruments and taught him the chants for all the idols. 1000 is the cube of Ten, a symbol of perfection.

Potiphar's wife tempted Joseph with 1000 talents of silver, when her personal charms failed to move him.

The thickness of the earth's crust is 1000 ells: below this is an abyss of 15,000 ells. Succah, 53. 2.

If you have a secret, tell it only to One in 1000.

1004. B.C. The Consecration of Solomon's Temple.

1081. The number of Tiphereth, the central Sephira, the Sun, Beauty, Microprosopus, Sun-God.

1263. The number of the word Gnosis.

1271. He Gnosis, The Gnosis, and Stauros, the cross of Jesus.

1322. First year of Egyptian cycle of Sothis, B.C.; Rameses II. came to the throne in this year, B.C.

1378. The reputed year of the birth of Christian Rosenkreutz, founder of the Rosicrucian philosophy.

1408. Christian Rosenkreutz founded his arcane society in Germania.

1459. The date of the writing of the Hermetic Romance of the Chemical Wedding, by C. R.

1461. The Egyptian Sothic Period, calculated by the heliacal rising of Sirius, the Dog Star, at the solstice.

1480. Christos, in Greek numeration: meaning Anointed: according to "The Canon" this number exhibits an important measure of the Cosmos, and was the foundation of the scientific pantheism upon which Christian theology was built, it was a part of The Gnosis and was derived from the priestly astronomers of Egypt.

1484. Christian Rosenkreutz died: the Vault closed over his body and the secrets of the Order he had founded.

1604. The Vault of C. R. opened by his successors after 120 years of secret study and benevolence.

1614. The Fama Fraternitatis Rosæ Crucis was printed.

1717. Grand Lodge of Freemasons was founded.

1752. New Year's Day changed from March 25 to January 1.

1865. Frater Robert Wentworth Little founded the Rosicrucian Society of Freemasons of England, in its present form.

1885. Dr. Wm. Robert Woodman became Supreme Magus.

1892. Dr. Wm. Wynn Westcott became Supreme Magus.

1911. This year A.D. is the 5013th year of the Kali-Yuga of the Hindoo sages; this Yuga is to continue 432,000 years.

2000. A Sabbath day's journey was 2000 paces. Rabbi Gamaliel had a tube made which, when he looked through, he could see objects at 2000 cubits distance; this is the earliest suggestion of the telescope. Eiruvin, 43. 2.

2368. The Greek number of Iesous Christos.

3000. Rav Hammunah says that Solomon spoke 3000 proverbs. At the mourning for Moses 3000 precepts were forgotten.

3102. In B.C. 3102, in February the Kali Yuga, the Black Age of humanity began, according to the Brahmins.

3761. The Jewish Era was calculated to commence 3761 years before the Christian Era.

4231 Years after the dispersion, said Rashi, the Jews will be restored to their own land.

4291. After these years the wars of Gog and Magog will cease, says the Talmud.

5888. The number of verses in the Pentateuch, says the Kiddushin: but they are usually counted as 5845.

6000. The world was intended to last 6000 years: woo years of Disorder; 2000 of the Law: and woo more before Messiah should come; but his Coming has been delayed by our iniquities; so says the Talmudic treatise. Sanhedrin, 97. 1.

25,000. According to Ezekiel the mystical city of Jerusalem was surrounded by a square space measuring 25,000 roods in length, and this he called The Holy Oblation, and it was for the use of the priests, the sons of Zadok.

3.14159, the value of ir, the ratio of diameter to circumference of a circle.

Bode's Law is a curious arithmetical and astronomical problem:—

Take the series of numbers   0 3   6 12 24 48   96 192
Add 4 to each of them   4 4   4   4   4   4   4   4
And we obtain the numbers   4 7 10 16 28 52 100 196

These show the relation of the ancient planets to the Sun, as to distance, in the order Mercury, Venus, Earth, Mars, Jupiter, Saturn, Uranus. The planet corresponding to 28 is missing, and seems to be replaced by the asteroids. Uranus was discovered in 1781.

The Platonic Year, or great Period, according to Tycho Brahé, is 25,816 years; Ricciolus, 25,920 years; Cassini, 24,800 years; Norman Lockyer now gives 24,450 years.

It is the period of time determined by the revolution of the equinoxes, or the space of time wherein the stars and constellations return to their former places in respect to the equinoxes by means of a constant precession. The equinoxes moving backwards or westwards, meet the Sun constantly earlier. In the time of the oldest Greek observations, the equinoxial points were in the first stars of Aries and Libra respectively; they are now in Pisces and Virgo. When these names were given the sun entered Aries at the Vernal equinox, and Sign and constellation coincided; now they do not, so do not be confused by our still calling the first Sign of spring Aries, although the Sun is now really at such time in Pisces: every 2160 years the Sign is changed. Precedent to Aries the Sun at the Vernal equinox entered Taurus.

THE APOCALYPTIC NUMBERS.

1st Resurrection, Revelation xx. 5.

2nd Death, xx. 14. 2 Witnesses, xi. 3.

2 Olive Trees, 2 Candlesticks before throne of God of the Earth, xi. 4.

2-Horned Beast who spoke like a Dragon, xiii. 11; his number is 666.

3 Woes, ix. 12.

1/3 part of Vegetation killed, viii. 7-do. of Sea became Blood, and do. of Fish died, viii. 8-do. of Waters became bitter, viii. 11-do. of Sun, Moon, Stars, viii. 12.

3½ days, Bodies lay unburied, xxi. 9.

4 quarters of the Earth, xx. 8.

4 Beasts, full of eyes and have 6 wings, iv. 6–9 ("Beasts" should be *living beings*.—W.).

4 Horses, White, Red, Pale, Black.

4 Horns of the golden altar before God, ix. 13.

4 Angels of the Euphrates, ix. 14.

4 Angels of the Winds of the 4 corners of the Earth, vii. 1.

5 Months the Locusts had power to hurt Men, ix. 5–10.

6 Wings of the Beasts (living beings), full of eyes, iv. 8.

7 Churches, i. 20.

7 Candlesticks, i. 20. Represent the 7 Churches.

7 Stars, i. 20; ii. 1. Represent 7 angels of the Churches.

7 Angels of the Churches, i. 20.

7 Lamps stand near the Throne, iv. 5.

7 Seals, v. 5, opened by the Lamb, produce 4 horses, etc.

7 Trumpets, viii. 2. Given to 7 Angels.

7 Thunders utter their voices, x. 3.

7 Plagues held by 7 Angels, xv. 1.

7 Vials of Wrath, xv. 7.

7 Spirits of God, v. 6.

7-horned and 7-eyed Lamb, v. 6; near the Throne are the 7 Spirits of God.

7-headed and 10-horned Scarlet Beast, on which is a Woman, xvii. 3.

7-headed and 10-horned Dragon with 7 Crowns, xii. 3.

7-headed and 10-horned Beast rose out of Sea, xiii. 1.

10 Crowns on Ten horns of beast which had 7 heads, xiii. 1.

10-horned Dragon with 7 heads, xii. 3.

10-horned Beast with 7 heads rose out of sea, xiii. 1.

10-horned Scarlet Beast with 7 heads, on which was a woman, xvii. 3.

12 Tribes of Israel.

12 Apostles of the Lamb, xxi. 14.

12 Gates of the New Jerusalem, 12 Angels guarding them xxi. 12.

12 Foundations of the Walls of the New Jerusalem.

12 Stars on the head of the Woman, xii. 1.

12 sorts of Fruit on the Tree of Life, xxii. 2.

24 Elders around the Throne, on 24 seats, iv. 4–10.

42 months the Gentiles tread over the outer court of Temple, xi. 2.

42 months the 7-headed Beast to have power to blaspheme, xiii. 5.

144 cubits, the height of the Walls of the New Jerusalem, xxi. 17.

666, the number of "The Beast."

1000 years, the Dragon bound for, xx. 2–3.

1000 years, Souls of the Faithful to live and reign, xx. 4.

1260 days, the two Witnesses prophesy, xi. 3.

1260 days, the Woman to be in the wilderness, xii. 6. 12,000 of each Tribe chosen.

12,000 furlongs, length of the sides of the New Jerusalem, xxi. 16.

144,000 chosen from the whole of the Tribes.

100,000,000, or ten thousand times ten thousand Angels, round the Throne, v. 11.

Made in the USA
Las Vegas, NV
12 February 2024

85714647R00056